Fashion Design for Living

Fashion Design for Living explores the positive contribution that the contemporary fashion designer can make within society. The book seeks to reveal new ways of designing and making fashion garments and products that not only enhance and enrich our lives, but also are mindful of social and sustainable issues.

This book sets out to question and challenge the dominant, conventional process of fashion design that as a practice has been under-researched. While the fashion designer in industry is primarily concerned with the creation of the new seasonal collection, designed, produced and measured by economically driven factors, society increasingly expects the designer to make a positive contribution to our social, environmental and cultural life. Consequently an emergent set of designers and research-based practitioners are beginning to explore new ways to think about fashion designing. The contributors within this book argue that fashion designing should move beyond developing garments that are just aesthetically pleasing or inexpensive, and begin to consider and respond to the wearer's experiences, wellbeing, problems, desires and situations, and their engagement with and use of a garment.

Fashion Design for Living champions new approaches to fashion practice by uncovering a rich and diverse set of views and reflective experiences which explore the changing role of the fashion designer and inspire fresh, innovative and creative responses to fashion and the world we live in.

Alison Gwilt is a fashion design academic, consultant and researcher exploring the integration of sustainable strategies across the lifecycle of fashion products. Her work focuses on the use of positive/sustainable design interventions within the fashion industry that challenge the current production and consumption paradigm. She has published widely in the field of sustainability and fashion, and her outputs include books, chapters, conference papers and articles published in the press and a number of international publications. Alison is Reader in Fashion and Sustainability at Sheffield Hallam University, UK.

'*Fashion Design for Living* provides wide-ranging case studies and diverse approaches to design for sustainability centred on the user experience of clothing and fashion, with a special focus on personal wellbeing, emotional engagement and collaborative design practice. The book is a valuable addition to resources for students and professionals on fashion and sustainability.'

Professor Sandy Black, Centre for Sustainable Fashion,
University of the Arts London, UK.
Author/Editor *The Sustainable Fashion Handbook;
Eco Chic: The fashion paradox*

'The call is clear. We need to think in new ways as we address current fashion challenges. By focusing on the wellbeing of people, through a user-centered design approach, innovative solutions will be found. This array of timely and inspiring essays is a solid start; read it and take action.'

Janet Hethorn, Director, Delaware Design Institute,
University of Delaware, USA

Fashion Design for Living

Edited by
Alison Gwilt

Routledge
Taylor & Francis Group

LONDON AND NEW YORK

First published 2015
by Routledge
2 Park Square, Milton Park, Abingdon, Oxon OX14 4RN

and by Routledge
711 Third Avenue, New York, NY 10017

Routledge is an imprint of the Taylor & Francis Group, an informa business

British Library Cataloguing-in-Publication Data
A catalogue record for this book is available from the British Library

Library of Congress Cataloging-in-Publication Data
Fashion design for living / edited by Alison Gwilt.
pages cm
Includes index.
1. Fashion design. I. Gwilt, Alison.
TT507.F3484 2015
746.9'2--dc23
2014014272

ISBN: 978-0-415-71771-7 (hbk)
ISBN: 978-0-415-71772-4 (pbk)
ISBN: 978-1-315-77075-8 (ebk)

Typeset in Bembo
by Saxon Graphics Ltd, Derby

Printed by Bell and Bain Ltd, Glasgow

Contents

Contents

Contents

List of figures

List of contributing authors

Joe Au is currently Associate Professor at the Institute of Textiles and Clothing, the Hong Kong Polytechnic University. He received his AAS degree in Fashion Design from the Fashion Institute of Technology (FIT), State University of New York, USA, in 1991 and Master's degree in Design Theory/History and Design Management from the College of Fine Arts, the University of New South Wales, Australia, in 1998. He then obtained his PhD in Fashion Design from the Hong Kong Polytechnic University in 2003. His research interests include fashion design theory, creative garment pattern cutting and wearable electronics.

Ricarda Bigolin is a designer, lecturer and researcher in the Fashion Program at RMIT University, Melbourne, Australia. She was awarded her PhD by project, entitled 'Undo Fashion: Loose Garment Practice', in 2012. Her practice is concerned with critical and expanded approaches to fashion design that question and explore fashion production and the allusive and aspirational qualities of high and luxury fashion. A continual investigation and critique of the strategies of fashion branding is expressed notably in practice and projects involving collaboration and outputs across various fields. Her research, design and teaching practice encourage the extension of fashion design thinking through such modes of expression as writing, exhibition, film and performance.

Kate Carroll is Assistant Professor at the College of Textiles at North Carolina State University, USA. She teaches Fashion Design and Product Development classes. She is interested in product development issues that are not typically found in ready-to-wear fashion. She is also interested in clothing as material culture and historic inspiration for contemporary design. She runs a website called Fashioning Health and Well-Being. Dr Carroll received a BA in Art History from the University of Manchester, UK, an MA in Costume and Textiles from Michigan State University, USA, and a PhD from Virginia Tech, USA.

Joan Farrer is Director of the Design Research Initiatives (DR–i). Her research expertise stems from a deep working knowledge of the industrial retail sector and R&D in fashion, textiles, fibre and materials design and global supply and disposal chain knowledge. Her sustainable and 'smart' transdisciplinary research collaborations include, apart from the arts, physical and biomedical science, computing, mathematics and engineering. She advises on policy to industrial, governmental and non-governmental organizations and educational institutions. Her Royal College of Art PhD, awarded without amendments in 2000, was acclaimed as one of the first in fashion textile global supply chain analysis.

Angela Finn is Senior Lecturer in Design at AUT University in Auckland, New Zealand. As a designer and maker, her published research – which covers sustainable design, health and wellbeing, practitioner research, tacit knowledge in fashion and tacit knowledge transfer – centres on the role of the design practitioner within the changing landscape of the fashion industry, contemporary fashion research and the modern education system as it relates to fashion education. At the time of writing, Angela's PhD thesis, entitled 'Designing Fashion: An Exploration of Practice-led Research within the Academic Environment' is under final examination.

Alison Gwilt is a fashion design academic, consultant and researcher exploring the integration of sustainable strategies across the lifecycle of fashion products. Her work focuses on the use of positive/sustainable design interventions within the fashion industry that challenge the current production and consumption paradigm. She has published widely in the field of sustainability and fashion, and her outputs include books, chapters, conference papers and articles published in the press and a number of international publications. Alison is Reader in Fashion and Sustainability at Sheffield Hallam University, UK.

Eunjeong Jeon, a Korean interaction designer and researcher, has her base in Western Australia. She studied at the Danish Institute for Study Abroad (DIS) in 1996; Hongik University College of Fine Arts, Seoul, South Korea (BA, 1997); and Curtin University, Western Australia (MA, 2005), where she also received her PhD (2013). She has participated in numerous art and industry projects, workshops, conferences, design debates and international exhibitions, and was invited to work as a Postdoctoral Researcher in Industrial Design at Eindhoven University of Technology (TU/e), the Netherlands (2012–2013).

Jin Lam is currently a tutor at the Institute of Textiles and Clothing, the Hong Kong Polytechnic University. She received her BA (Hons) in Fashion and Textiles (first class honours), majoring in Fashion Design, and MA in Fashion and Textile Design (distinction), both from the Hong Kong Polytechnic University, in 2007 and 2008 respectively. She then obtained her PhD in Fashion Design from the Hong Kong Polytechnic University in 2012; the topic of her doctorate thesis is 'Creation of Illuminative Smart Fashion'. Her research interests include a wide range of topics including fashion design, fashion illustration and wearable electronics.

Lydia Lavín is Director and Designer of her own contemporary Mexican fashion brand, Lydia Lavín. Since studying at the Universidad Iberoamericana in Mexico City, Parsons School of Design in New York, USA, and Istituto Marangoni and Scuola di Disegno in Italy, Lavín has worked for almost 30 years as a Professor in Textile Design at the Universidad Iberoamericana. Her research work with the National Indigenous Institute focused on the preservation of indigenous garments, and she has undertaken a number of collaborations with the National Institute of Fine Arts (Mexico) and Fomento Cultural Banamex. As a designer Lavín's mission is to establish a sustainable business that encourages the traditions of the artisan.

Montserrat Messeguer Lavín is a textile and fashion designer, and co-designer at the prestigious Mexican fashion house Lydia Lavín, in which she creates textiles using experimental techniques and in collaborations with artisans from all over Mexico, as well as designing the ready-to-wear line. She studied at FIT (the Fashion Institute of Technology) in New York and the Paris American Academy, and graduated from Universidad Iberoamericana in Mexico in 2011. She has been the recipient of prizes including a Pierre Cardin Scholarship (2010) and the National Textile Talent Award (2012) of the Textile and Fashion Chamber of Mexico, and has worked for fashion and textile consultants Asesortex.

Jane McCann was Director of the Smart Clothes and Wearable Technology research group (University of South Wales, UK, 2004–2012), where she led cross-disciplinary research culminating in her role as Principal Investigator of the New Dynamics of Ageing collaborative research project Design for Ageing

Well, looking into 'improving the quality of life of the ageing population using a technology enabled garment system'. She launched the unique MA Performance Sportswear Design programme at the University of Derby (1995) that provided the international sports industry with designers, many still in key positions today. McCann was awarded the Sir Misha Black Award for Innovation in Design Education in 2004.

Daijiro Mizuno studied for an MA and PhD in Fashion Design at the Royal College of Art (RCA), UK, while working for Shelley Fox during the period 2000–2003. Since graduating from the RCA in 2008 Daijiro has lived and worked primarily in Japan, studying and practising design research relating to the creativity of the 'savage' designers in the wild. He is an Associate Professor in the Faculty of Environment and Information Studies at Keio University, Japan, and a Specially Appointed Senior Lecturer at Kyoto University Design School, Japan. He has published several books in Japanese including *Fashionista* and *Vanitas*, a fashion critique magazine. www.daijirom.com

Adam Thorpe is co-founder and design partner of London-based Vexed Generation/Vexed Design. He is also a Reader in Socially Responsive Design at Central Saint Martins, University of the Arts London, UK, where he is co-director of the Design Against Crime (DAC) Research Centre and coordinator of the Socially Responsive Design and Innovation research group and the Design for Social Innovation and Sustainability (DESIS) Lab. His research activities are practice-based and explore the role of design(ers) in collaborative address of societal goals and challenges.

Foreword

When we started testing solutions to the problem of design for a seated body, we had little idea that this would make us somewhat special. It was just a problem that needed a solution. The fashion industry created garments with a distinct lack of functionality for people outside the stand-up norm. The disability industry had a severely impaired fashion sense. And we enjoyed problem solving.

In hindsight, it is clear that several choices we made in the early days would make us special: the solutions should be provided free of charge; the knowledge of how to achieve them should be presented so even a beginner understood; and any functional aspects should be for the wearer's benefit – not for the person assisting with dressing or undressing. For us, clothes should represent the personality of the wearer, and possibly signal cultural, political or group affiliation if so wanted. Our aim has always been to empower the individual and it is, after all, individuals that make up the fabric of our social, environmental and cultural life.

Maybe a truly sustainable fashion is the sort that adapts and shifts, changes shape and expression after the individual wearer's needs and wants? Maybe the design process should have its main location on the individual body?

Trying to adapt already existing garments is a liberating process. You learn to think outside the box when the umpteenth trial, to enable movement for a wheelchair user's propelling arms while keeping a winter jacket in place, miserably fails. The perspective shifts and the problem reformulates itself. What was a problem of how to increase flexibility in winter jackets is suddenly a question of how to keep the upper body functionally and fashionably warm. Warmth is generated by sleeves and bodies, collars and hoods, gloves, arm warmers, scarves, and more. Nobody really needs them to come in pre-packed combinations. Why not just pick and mix?

Maybe the truly avant-garde fashion is the one enabling everyone to be their very own designer? Maybe empowering the wearer, by providing choices – not just how a dress looks but what constitutes a dress – can be defined as design for living? It might mean that this season's pieces will remain largely unsold while the op-shop (charity shop) bought jacket gets its sleeves chopped off. Why not see this too as a liberating process?

The chapters in this anthology are full of promise and it is a pleasure to realize that there are so many interesting ideas and activities going on within the fashion world today. It is indeed our privilege to scribble some of our thoughts into its pages. It is a great start, but in the future we would like to see the remit expanded even further, to challenge, not just the conventional process of fashion design, but what constitutes fashion and why wearers need to be grouped according to categories.

Susanne and Meagan
for FashionFreaks
http://en.fashionfreaks.se

Acknowledgements

I would like to thank the authors Adam Thorpe, Joan Farrer and Angela Finn, Jane McCann, Lydia Lavín and Montserrat Messeguer Lavín, Ricarda Bigolin, Daijiro Mizuno, Eunjeong Jeon, Kate Carroll, Jin Lam and Joe Au for their valuable contributions. I would also like to thank Susanne Berg and Meagan Whellans (FashionFreaks) for providing an insightful foreword.

I also wish to thank: Trudy Varcianna at Routledge for her support; Laura Williamson for her enthusiasm for the proposal; and Todd Robinson at University of Technology, Sydney for discussions that inspired the book's inception.

Finally, I would like to thank Ian and Dylan for their continued love and support.

Introduction

Fashion Design for Living explores the different positive contributions that the fashion designer can make within society. It attempts to discuss new ways to approach fashion designing, and specifically the ways in which fashion products and services can enhance and enrich our lives.

Traditionally, commercial and economic factors, rather than the issues and problems of contemporary life, have driven the fashion creative process. In general, the mainstream fashion industry continues to rate the success of a garment simply on its aesthetic value, and it is the aesthetics-based value system that contributes to the view that fashion is superfluous. However, there is an opportunity for fashion to make a positive contribution in society. Increasingly fashion designers are becoming aware of the need to tackle the environmental and ethical impacts associated with production and consumption, and while these tentative steps, which often revolve around developing more environmentally/ethically sensitive production processes, are to be applauded, it is fashion's broader engagement with society – particularly marginalized groups of people – that remains difficult. Fashion is a highly visual form of personal expression and it is through the wearing of fashion garments that individuals can express their values, interests and identity. For many people a relationship with fashion is important because it enhances independence and confidence and provides a sense of wellbeing. From this perspective there is unquestionably value in the aesthetic qualities of a fashion garment, but it is evident within the chapters of this book that while aesthetics play an important part there are other considerations that can be taken into account. However, for fashion designers to become more responsive to these social value

1

systems there needs to be a collective engagement and sharing of responsibilities between producers, designers, wearers and other stakeholders/communities.

Within this book the chapters question and challenge the traditional fashion production–consumption paradigm and reveal models that enable the development of products and services that support individual and social enhancement. The contributing authors describe user-centred approaches and practices that provide the opportunity for wearers to respond to, engage with and participate in the creative process. Each author provides a different perspective on how fashion design can positively contribute to our social, environmental and cultural existence. These accounts uncover a variety of approaches that focus on users, lived experiences and actual and everyday problems or scenarios, which often remain unfamiliar or adjacent to the fashion design process applied in industry or in the educational fashion design studio. *Fashion Design for Living* champions new approaches to fashion practice, through a rich and diverse set of views and reflective experiences, which aim to inspire fresh, innovative and creative responses to the world around us.

Separated into two parts, the book begins with an exploration of the notion of 'fashion for existence'. The chapters in this first section examine the different methodologies in design practice that attempt to improve the quality of our present and future lives and environments. Adam Thorpe, in Chapter 1, discusses his approach to design in relation to the work of the company Vexed Generation/ Vexed Design, which he co-founded with Joe Hunter. Thorpe's practice is driven by the belief that fashion design can be socially responsive, and his chapter provides an insight into the way in which designers can work with users and other stakeholders to develop products and/or processes that serve to highlight issues of concern. Joan Farrer and Angela Finn, in Chapter 2, examine the opportunities for fashion and textile designers to improve our health and wellbeing while working from within a transdisciplinary team. This approach, for Farrer and Finn, has helped facilitate the development of new fashion products that reduce the impacts of sun damage on human health. In Chapter 3, Jane McCann discusses the importance of adopting an inclusive design approach to fashion design as a method for developing products for an ageing population, something of significance to us all. McCann highlights the benefits that fashion can provide if we include users in the creative process. The notion of being resourceful in fashion design at a time when our natural resources are being depleted is explored in the next chapter. In this chapter (Chapter 4) I outline some of the attitudes and practices of wearers towards clothing repair in contemporary society, and discuss approaches that designers can utilize to encourage wearers to (re-)engage with clothing repair strategies. Finally in this section, in Chapter 5, Lydia Lavín and Montserrat Messeguer Lavín discuss the relationship that they have established with textiles artisans in indigenous communities in Mexico. Through the 'Lydia Lavín' fashion label the designers set out to preserve traditional textile craftsmanship and support local livelihoods.

Part 2 explores fashion for engagement, and the chapters in this section propose approaches that enable and support people to engage in or participate with fashion. The section begins with Ricarda Bigolin's examination (Chapter 6) of imagined fashion products as a way to encourage participation and social engagement. Bigolin's approach intends to challenge notions of exclusiveness that dominate many aspects of fashion practice. In Chapter 7, Daijiro Mizuno discusses the shift that can occur within the creative process if we engage wearers through open design and digital fabrication processes. Through these processes, Mizuno proposes that the fashion designer can act as a social agent, empowering wearers to engage with multiple layers of customization in fashion. Eunjeong Jeon, in Chapter 8, draws on experiential bodily knowing and understanding as a way to develop new garment forms. Jeon's work specifically explores comfort in clothing, by investigating the influence of the tactile (haptic) experience, kinaesthetic interaction and emotion. In Chapter 9, Kate Carroll adopts a universal design approach to fashion design that promotes an improved engagement for wearers with physical disabilities. Carroll's analysis of the design and development process, including user interactions, testing and evaluation periods, demonstrate the real value ascribed to understanding other perspectives. To conclude, Jin Lam and Joe Au, in Chapter 10, discuss the potential of fashion garments to sense and react to changes in our environments, through the use of wearable technologies. The authors propose that in the future wearers may be able to interact visually through clothing, in ways that complement, differentiate, expand or enrich other human approaches to communication.

Fashion Design for Living provides a critical platform that encourages the fashion designer to move beyond developing products chiefly for their aesthetic qualities and instead create products/services that more actively bring wearers' needs and experiences into play. In these scenarios it is critical that fashion *should* engage wearers if there is to be a successful shift in cultural attitudes and behaviours towards clothing consumption. By embracing the types of engagement outlined in this book we have a real opportunity for change.

Alison Gwilt

PART I
_____

FASHION FOR EXISTENCE

Chapter One

Fashioning publics

The socially responsive design practice of Vexed Generation

Adam Thorpe, Vexed Generation/Vexed Design and Central Saint Martins, University of the Arts London, UK

Socially responsive design has been defined as 'Design that takes as its primary driver social issues, its main consideration social impact and its main objective social change' (Gamman and Thorpe 2006). It is also the term that clothing designers Vexed Generation used to describe the kind of clothing and product design we delivered in London in the 1990s that took as its inspiration the social and environmental concerns of the day.

Whilst the above definition of socially responsive design successfully articulates a shared agenda with 'socially useful design' (Whiteley 1993), describing a design process applied in order to address social needs and human wellbeing over and above stimulating human desires so as to drive market economies, it fails to explain the intended distinction between socially *responsive* design and socially *responsible* design that is key to articulating a practice which understands responsibility as an 'ability to respond' (Derrida 1983).

The distinction is twofold, linked to i) the relationship of socially responsive design to the market, as expressed by Morelli (2007): 'the time has come to review Papanek … from a new perspective which reduces the distance between market-based and socially oriented initiatives', and ii) the agency of designers over design processes and designed products, in both their creation and use. As existing debates in the field reflect (Papanek 1985; Rittel and Webber 1973; Buchanan 1992; Morelli 2007), socially *responsive* design does not acknowledge the primacy of designers as *responsible* for the societal outcomes related to the processes and products of design. Instead, socially *responsive* design understands design for society as a socially 'situated practice' akin to Suchman's concept of 'situated action'

(Suchman 1987), in that it is contingent on the situated context of the design process, particularly the agency of the people in and around it. The ability of design to have social impact in use is similarly contingent on users and contexts and, ultimately, beyond the control of the designer in that designs 'are constituted through and inseparable from the specifically situated practices of their use' (Suchman *et al.* 1999).

This is not to say that socially responsive design rejects the notion of designers seeking to make responsible decisions as regards the impacts of their practices and products on social systems. Rather it suggests that when design is delivered via commission or collaboration the designers' agency over the process and its outcomes is not entire. This is not a shortcoming of design, in the context of socially useful design and/or design-led social innovation, but a condition of it. Socially responsive design is socially situated in process and in product – throughout the design's lifecycle – and as designers we are only able to be *responsive* rather than ultimately *responsible* in our engagement with social, political and ethical agendas and objectives.

In this way socially responsive design seeks to offer a pragmatic reading of social design practice that does not require designers to eschew consumerism and the market to deliver socially motivated and mindful design.

The following case studies describe two initiatives delivered by Vexed Generation/Vexed Design between 1993 and 2003. They will, it is hoped, illustrate a fashion design practice that is socially responsive in both its means (the process of design) and its ends (the products of design). They seek to demonstrate how designers of clothing and accessories can attempt to achieve socially responsive practice by application of different methodologies offering, in different intensities, social and market oriented activity and collaboration with the users and stakeholders of their designs.

'You put up a camera and I'll put up a collar': Vexed Generation clothing between 1993 and 1995

When Joe Hunter and I started designing clothes together in 1993 as Vexed Generation we knew we could not compete in the fashion industry, and we did not want to.

We knew that our meagre resources (we were both on the dole for the most part when we started Vexed) and limited training and industry experience (neither of us had a formal fashion training) meant we could not compete on price (other brands would always benefit from economies of scale and cheaper overseas manufacture we could not and did not wish to achieve); quality (we had limited experience of designing and manufacturing clothing and so did not assume that we could do so 'better' than those who had been at it for years); or marketing (we had no resources to pay for PR or advertising to spread awareness of or generate desire for our creations).

Nor were we preoccupied with making clothes that we thought were 'on trend' or 'in fashion' and would therefore be desirable to consumers. Constantly trawling the markets and charity shops of Camden, Portobello and Brick Lane, we were painfully aware of – and disparaging of – the manner in which the styles adopted and adapted by the patrons of these stalls were aped in subsequent seasons by fashion brands in what we saw as an ever-decreasing spiral of creativity and quality. The 'new' versions of these garments were of such inferior quality of material and manufacture that they would never make it back to the market stall for re-sale and re-use but rather contribute to landfill, resource use and climate change.

Consequently we sought to make clothing that was unlike any other. Clothing that met the contemporary personal and social needs of people like us living in London at the time. To do this we asked different questions of our clothing in an attempt to find different sartorial answers and we embraced the aesthetics that these answers suggested, even when they appeared odd and incongruous.

We wanted to make our clothes in the UK, for the UK and about the UK.

In the UK

Our desire to manufacture in the UK was not a consequence of nationalism but because we wished to contribute to jobs and prosperity locally if we were able. We also held perhaps romantic and misplaced ideals linked to the sustenance, even prosperity, of skilled labour, craftsmanship and artisanship within UK clothing and accessory manufacture. By manufacturing clothing that was 'beautiful and useful' (Morris 1880) in the UK we hoped to assure a future for workers seeking to experience the inherent self-expression, satisfaction and reward of a job well done. This perspective is more clearly articulated by Sennett (2008) in his exploration of craftsmanship. Certainly, as newcomers to the skills and competencies required to make clothing that would endure, we were respectful of, even enamoured with, those who could realise our design prototypes as desirable and marketable products of a quality that would last. We anticipated that this durability, physical and emotional (Chapman 2005), would avoid the necessity to contribute to the un-merry-go-round of resource depletion and landfill engendered by the disposable fashion of which we were critical.

We were also keen to play a role in maintaining a regional diversity in fashion, such as the style defined by Breward *et al.* (2004) as a 'London Look'. We consciously sought to offer an alternative to the homogenised aesthetics of globalisation that were losing their appeal for a generation of taste makers that were part of a 90s DIY creative culture, a culture fostered in part by digital democratisation (of music and film) and in part by a recessionary economic climate. This same climate created redundant capacity in space and labour that meant that we could find (and just about afford) studio space, factory space and retail space to get our small dockets into production and distribution.

For and about the UK

In London, in 1993, the Conservative government tabled the Criminal Justice bill. Amongst a raft of wide ranging proposals, the bill sought to introduce new legislation granting additional powers to the police that specifically targeted certain practices and lifestyles in UK culture, including raves (free outdoor parties); squatting (living free and without permission in unoccupied property); 'unauthorised camping' on public land; and much peaceful outdoor protest (particularly environmental protest, which often involved occupation of land to prevent socially and environmentally harmful activities being carried out by the authorities, for example road expansion schemes and inhumane animal testing and transportation). The bill also championed surveillance (the use of CCTV by local authorities). In effect the Criminal Justice bill sought to criminalise, and in so doing eradicate, many social and collaborative cultural practices that supported – and in some cases constituted – alternative lifestyles. Many, including Vexed Generation, perceived the bill as an attack on civil liberties and the ability of citizens to self-help in the face of social injustice and inequality. Furthermore, the partial and subjective nature of the legislation was perceived as indicative of an insidious and intolerant hegemony that would result in further marginalisation of certain groups within society. Despite fierce resistance, the bill was passed as an act in 1994.

The word *vexed* means 'annoyed', 'frustrated' or 'worried'. It also describes 'a problem or issue that is difficult, much debated and problematic'. The word *generation* describes 'all of the people born and living at about the same time, regarded collectively'. It also refers to 'the production or creation of something'. We considered the words *Vexed Generation* in several senses, simultaneously describing our state of mind in relation to social issues in London at the time and the broader cohort of likeminded people that shared them. They also related to the nature of our concerns and our intended action, our 'mission': to use these concerns to generate designs that would communicate and address them.

Consequently, Vexed Generation designed clothing that, it was observed, could 'simultaneously communicate these issues and protect their wearers from their worst effects' (Evans 2003).

Design research methodology

In the first instance we applied what could be regarded as an auto-ethnographic design research approach, though it was not understood as such at the time. As avid scooterists and cyclists we reflected on the shortcomings of the garments and accessories available to us; how could they facilitate less pollutive, and more accessible, approaches to urban mobility? Living in the London Borough of Tower Hamlets at the time, we were exposed to the early use of CCTV as it spread from its early application within the City of London's counter terrorist 'ring of steel' into the adjacent neighbourhoods. We conducted a literature review, grateful for the assistance of friendly journalists with access to Reuters news text (we had little or no access to the internet), who provided facts and figures on air quality and CCTV use as well as news of the ongoing activities surrounding the new powers introduced by the Criminal Justice Act (CJA). We carried out user-centred research, observing interactions between police and protesters, including police arrest techniques, on video and *in situ*. We engaged in 'immersive' design research, placing ourselves in situations that enabled us to experience these interactions further first hand – some willingly, some not so! We met with groups that were directly affected and engaged by the new legislation (JUSTICE, Liberty, Advance Party Network,[1] the Legal Defence and Monitoring Group, Privacy International), listening to their experiences and insights and discussing our proposals. We iteratively reviewed our findings and created a design framework (summarised in Figure 1.1) that informed our design development.

Social issues	Design themes	Design considerations
Air quality	Mobility	Freedom of movement
Civil liberties (CJA)	Privacy	Comfort
Surveillance (CCTV)	Protection	Durability
		Adaptability
		Concealed identity
		Concealed storage
		Physical protection
		Respiratory protection
		Weather protection
		Wearable communication

Figure 1.1: Table summarising the design framework.

Design development and production

These design considerations informed iterative product development that included sketching and 'paper' prototyping (including an early bag design prototyped in plastic bags and Sellotape). Pattern development and toile development followed. These product developments were informed by text books (Aldrich 1994); trial and error; capable friends with whom we shared studio space; and deconstruction and examination of our own collection of favourite garments, many of which were military clothing. Later iterations were sampled in low cost fabrics of weight and handle comparable to the preferred fabrics, and Joe and I wear-tested them. Final prototypes in comparable fabrics were further user-tested for several months by trusted friends (of similar but slightly different lifestyles and body shapes) and early customers, and pattern changes and product iterations made as necessary. Design decisions were informed by user feedback and our competency and knowledge of materials and construction techniques. One example of how these limitations shaped our design process was our penchant for Velcro, a fastening we favoured due to its versatility and ease of use, in production (straight stitch into place) and wear (good with gloves on) and the fact that it is easy to restore (clean with a pin) and replace (remove the panel and straight stitch on a new one). Our familiarity with Velcro significantly contributed to the originality of the design of the Vexed bag, which featured a Velcro strap closure. In parallel, and in response to the user-centred research described above, we also engaged in materials research. Materials were selected and developed for their performance characteristics, their language and meaning and finally their environmental impact. Sometimes there were conflicts between the required performance and language and the environmental impact of a material. In these instances Vexed prioritised social concerns (people) over environmental concerns (planet). The garments' performance and language in use would take precedence. Our consideration of environment was implicit in the durability of the garments and their impact in use, for example advocating and enabling urban mobility other than the use of cars, and raising awareness of civil liberties, which impacted upon those who fought for environmental preservation. This contradiction was apparent to us at the time and informed the definition of our practice as socially *responsive* rather than socially *responsible*.

Finally, specified materials and prototypes were passed to manufacturers who consulted on the most appropriate production techniques (sometimes involving minor construction and pattern amendment) and production prototypes were developed, which were wear-tested prior to batch production.

Design outcomes

The Vexed Parka (1994) (Figure 1.2) from the first Vexed Generation collection clearly illustrates the way in which the 'brief', developed from the 'research', informed the 'design'.

The Parka was the collection's 'flagship' piece. The design directly responded to all the issues highlighted in the 'brief': civil liberties (CJA), air pollution and CCTV. The Parka parodies police riot gear in aesthetic, material performance and material language. We were happy if the appearance was challenging, and hopeful that this challenge would receive a response in the form of discussion and debate in the media and on the street – why was this garment relevant? We were conscious that the concerns we were seeking to communicate were not overt; noxious gases that contribute to respiratory illness, particularly amongst the old and young, are invisible except for their effects; CCTV is often squirrelled away from those it surveys; and civil liberties are more apparent in practice than in policy. In addressing these concerns the design of the Vexed Parka sought to make them visible.

The Parka was made from MOD grade, high tenacity ballistic nylon that is slash proof. This fabric had never previously been deployed in civilian street-wear and had previously been used primarily in bulletproof vests and 'blast curtains' (curtains that contain flying fragments during controlled explosions). We applied a fire

13

Figure 1.2: Vexed Parka (1994).

Photographers: Haraldur Hannes Gudasundsson (left); Jonny Thompson (right).

resistant neoprene coating to the fabric (though in later versions of the Parka we changed this for a waterproof breathable polyurethane coating, as the neoprene proved to make the wearer hot and sweaty). The Parka includes strategically placed protective padding throughout the crown, spine, kidney and groin areas (areas one might get struck with a baton if in the wrong place at the wrong time). The hood and collar are designed to hide the wearer's face and accommodate a respiratory mask that is stored in a covered pocket on the sleeve of the garment (the pocket leaves part of the mask open to the air to enable condensation that has built up during use to evaporate away). The distinctive 'tail', front and back, joins between the legs to negate the effects of the 'groin grab' often deployed by police when making a street arrest (such as those made at parties and protests) to bring an individual into the 'stack' position (where a person is brought to their knees and their hands are brought behind their back to incapacitate them and allow for handcuffs to be applied). The chest pockets conceal a 'Velcro' lattice that enables items to be easily stowed and accessed.

Vexed retail

We started to seek retailers for our designs in 1995. Early direct sales to 'friends of friends' made us aware that our designs would be relevant to and popular with a wider public. Despite this we were unable to gain retail stockists or distribution. Feedback from retailers praised the 'intelligence' and 'originality' of the designs but feared their lack of precedent and felt they were 'not right for our customers'. Vexed pieces were often referred to as 'futuristic', a description that we found particularly frustrating given that they were designed in response to a brief derived from the current social context. In this way Vexed products were viewed as *proleptic*, existing before their proper or historical time and anticipating and answering social concerns before they had been raised or understood by the majority. In short, they were perceived to be as alternative as the concerns they sought to champion. Whilst we conceded that our products were antagonistic to market hegemony we were convinced of their social relevance and value and felt that if more people could engage with the products more would share this view. To achieve this we had to open a 'shop'.

Collaborating with likeminded designers, artists and musicians, and with the assistance of an international aid charity, supportive neighbours, and landlords seeking to enliven their estate during recession, we negotiated reduced rent and rates to occupy a vacant central London property on a short term lease (a 'pop-up' shop). Vexed's 'retail installation' opened in December 1995. The space communicated the concerns the collection responded to through the design of the retail environment. The design aimed to challenge and inform: the upstairs was a sterile surveyed dystopia in which the clothing was displayed, the downstairs a creative and communal space with public access record decks and an 'alternative TV service' made up of video works contributed by members of the public and 'news' broadcasts from 'Undercurrents', an alternative news service reporting on the ongoing struggle against the implementation of the CJA.

'They're not taking the piss, we're giving it away': Karrysafe collection (2002)

Research and practice in Design Against Crime (DAC) started at Central Saint Martins (CSM) in 1999, led by Dr Lorraine Gamman. The DAC initiative, now a world leading research centre, explores new ways that design can contribute to the prevention of crime incidents and their wider harmful consequences. A large portion of crime is opportunistic. Building on theories of situational crime prevention (Clarke 2008) and crime prevention through environmental design (Crowe 2000; Armitage 2013), DAC posits that design that reduces opportunities for crime will reduce incidence of crime. It also maintains that crime prevention through design delivers communal benefits linked to reduced costs to the tax-payer (through reduced load on the criminal justice system – 'cops, courts and corrections') and personal benefits linked to reductions in victimisation and criminalisation. Consequently, DAC at CSM originated an extended model of user-centred design that includes considerations linked to the misuse and abuse of products within the design process. In this way DAC sought to facilitate design which discourages illegitimate users of products, such as thieves, whilst simultaneously promoting the desires and needs of legitimate users.

In 2000, official records for both the London region and the UK indicated that street crime, particularly the theft of bags for their contents and other mobile accessories such as mobile phones, had increased.[2] In 2002, the UK Home Office and the Design Council, keen to explore new ways to address the issue, commissioned the DAC initiative at CSM to deliver practice-led research into ways that design might respond. Dr Gamman and her team had already undertaken significant research into bag theft, consulting a broad range of stakeholders with expert knowledge of the issue (including criminologists from the Jill Dando Institute of Security and Crime Science at University College London; the Metropolitan Police; and networks of victims and ex-offenders) to understand and visualise exactly what was stolen and how. This research was made available to designers via a CD-ROM entitled 'In the Bag';[3] of particular value to designers are the 'frameworks' that help them understand the principles of crime prevention and think through design responses likely to succeed in preventing crime. Also, the visualisations of 'theft perpetrator techniques' clearly show designers how crimes are committed, including *dipping* (pickpocketing), *lifting* (theft of property from a static location), *grabbing* (robbery of property from a person) and *slashing* (cutting through the body of the bag to remove its contents).

The DAC team applied their research to the design of anti-theft bags working with staff and students at CSM. The resulting work was exhibited in the UK and Milan[4] in the hope of drawing attention to the issue of bag theft and the potential for design to contribute to its prevention. It was also the intention to explore the possibility of licensing the CSM anti-theft bag designs to accessory and luggage brands. Despite enthusiastic media coverage, the industry did not adopt the new designs, with one leading brand representative arguing that 'crime is not the job of design[;] it is the job of the police'. Consequently, Gamman approached Vexed Generation, as designers with a track record in accessory innovation and protective materials and an awareness and concern for social issues, with a proposal that they respond to DAC's bag theft research by designing a range of theft preventing bags and accessories.

Vexed reviewed the existing research information, gaining a clear understanding of the *what*, *why*, *where* and *how* of bag theft and also of the strengths and weaknesses of existing staff and student anti-theft bag design responses, considering the balance between ease of use and resistance to theft. Consultation workshops with an advisory group of experts on bag theft (who included police, criminologists, people who had experienced bag theft and a self-defence instructor) provided further insight into bag theft prevention and personal security. Workshops included the acting out of theft scenarios in which we alternated between the role of victim and offender in order to get a clearer idea of the physical realities of bag theft and the objects and human interactions that surround it. From these detailed explorations of both user and abuser perspectives emerged significant understandings that informed the design of a range of bags and accessories which provided defence against the most common theft MOs (modi operandi). Materials were researched and selected for their slash resistance, durability, weather proofing, flexibility, weight, aesthetic and suitability for 'needle construction' methods. The resulting products combined accommodation of user requirements with defence against bag theft.

Design outcomes

The Karrysafe Screamer laptop bag (Figure 1.3) demonstrates the way in which the research into bag theft informed original product development.

Featuring a 'carry front strap' (a strap construction that positions the bag to the wearer's front when carried, unless the wearer chooses to adapt the strap for side or back carriage, in which case the strap obscures the bag opening), the 'safety breakaway' (an adjustable strap fastening that 'breaks' apart under extreme tear strength and in doing so releases the bag from the wearer, stopping them being dragged to the floor, and triggers a 138 decibel attack alarm within the bag), a 'securing lanyard' (a retractable, lockable lanyard that allows a bag to be secured to an immovable object) and a 'combination zip lock', the bag is constructed from high tenacity nylon with a slash resistant polypropylene interlining. The bag can

Figure 1.3: Karrysafe Screamer laptop bag.
Photographer: Andrew G. Hobbs.

carry a laptop and accessories, papers and other equipment. It is resistant to *dipping*, *lifting*, *grabbing* and *slashing*. The bag takes its name from the inclusion of an anti-attack alarm that is triggered if the bag is snatched from the wearer's grasp. When the bag is violently tugged away from the wearer the strap will break and the alarm will sound. The concealed alarm is inaccessible to the thief and will continue to sound for up to two hours at 138 decibels – meaning the thief is likely to discard the bag (with its contents secured within by the combination zip lock) – until the owner returns to the screaming bag after it has been discarded and reconnects the breakaway strap.

Karrysafe branding and marketing

The name 'Karrysafe', chosen for the collection of theft resistant bags and accessories, was consciously overt in its security focus and lent itself to 'sub branding' that communicated the specific theft MOs against which the design features protected. 'Dipsafe', 'Liftsafe', 'Grabsafe' and 'Slashsafe' icons and labelling were featured on swing tags and at point of sale. In this way, the branding itself aimed to raise awareness amongst consumers about the theft techniques they should familiarise themselves with and guard against. Selfridges supported the introduction of the Karrysafe product range, launching the collection with a carousel and point of sale featuring a combination of fashion photography and awareness raising brand communication. The products were also promoted and sold via a website[5] that offered support and advice to the public concerning the issues surrounding street crime and personal security, providing links to partner organisations.

The Karrysafe project was intended to raise awareness, amongst consumers and in industry, of personal property theft and the complicity of design in granting opportunities for crime to happen. It was hoped that awareness of crime issues, and design's ability to address them, might lead to demand for such functionality amongst consumers, which in turn might be met by market supply. The desired ultimate outcome of this 'market interventionist' approach was to increase the anti-crime functionality of bags and accessories and to reduce both opportunities for crime and the number of people victimised or criminalised. So the Karrysafe product range's primary purpose was not to establish a commercially successful brand – although we were happy for the brand to be a commercial success – but rather to use commercial design intervention to establish a benchmark for crime resistant functionality that other designers and brands might incorporate into their own products in less overt ways.

From products and markets to 'things' and 'publics'

The above examples extend a user-centred approach to design to include consideration of other actors that impact upon, or are impacted upon by, the products and processes of design. For example, Vexed garments facilitated those that sought to enjoy activities and lifestyles legislated against by the CJA and threatened by the new powers it granted the police. Karrysafe designs aimed to deter thieves as well as meet the requirements of legitimate users of the bags. Consideration of 'actors' other than 'users' of the products has informed the development and application of design methodologies that go beyond design *for* users towards more participatory and collaborative design activities that involve designers in designing *with* users and other stakeholders.

This extended role and function of design and design process seeks to serve the 'users' of products (in the ways described above) whilst simultaneously highlighting the topics of concern that inspire the design response. In this way the products and processes of design provoke and focus conversation and debate, forming or extending a 'community of interest' (Fischer 2001) for the issues to which the design responds. The pragmatist philosopher John Dewey described such communities of concern as 'publics'. Rejecting the notion of the amorphous public, Dewey (1927) argued that a public comes into being around and through an issue of shared concern in order to address it. His thinking has informed many design researchers exploring the role of design in responding to social issues and shaping collaborative social action (Björgvinsson *et al.* 2010; DiSalvo 2009; DiSalvo *et al.* 2011; Thorpe and Gamman 2012; Malpass 2013; Binder *et al.* 2011). DiSalvo (2009) explores the 'designerly means for the identification and articulation of issues; such that they might be known enough to enable a public to form around them' and draws on the field of Critical Design as defined by Dunne (1998) to explain some of the design 'tactics' applied to do so. These include 'projection', which he describes as 'the representation of a possible set of future consequences associated with an issue' with the intention to 'make apparent the possible consequences of an issue' and 'tracing', which he defines as 'the use of designerly forms to detail and communicate, and to make known, the network(s) of materials, actions, concepts, and values that shape and frame an issue over time'. Whilst the cases detailed above apply such 'designerly means' to the articulation of social issues they also offer products which enable users to address these issues. In doing so these designs explicitly seek to be both 'public forming *and public serving*': public forming in that the product and/or process of design may facilitate or catalyse the formation of a community of interest 'on, around and through' the product and/or process; public serving in that the product and/or process of design facilitates a community of interest to *take action* in response to their concerns, to become a community of practice.

For example, the anonymising hood and military aesthetics of the Vexed Parka provoked conversation around the need for such a garment, catalysing debate and concern around civil liberties, surveillance and air quality whilst simultaneously concealing the wearer's identity and offering the protection they might need if they were demonstrating against perceived injustice or travelling around a polluted city. Similarly, the Karrysafe collection triggered debate around issues of personal theft and victimisation through the design and marketing of bags that protected their users from the various techniques of thieves.

It is these designs' implicit ability to facilitate socially responsive agency in use, their 'response-ability', facilitating 'an ability to respond' (Derrida 1983), that sets socially responsive design apart from critical design. Whilst critical designs may be speculative, challenging hegemony, articulating possible and alternative futures and facilitating the formation of publics 'on and around' them (Malpass 2013), they do not implicitly serve those publics in taking action to address the issues that concern them.

The cases discussed describe a socially responsive approach that 'informs, reforms and gives form' (Papanek 1995) *to* design and *through* design. Response to social issues informs, changes and shapes the process of design research, development and delivery as well as the aesthetic and function of the clothing designed. Ensuing response to the designs in 'use' is anticipated to inform, reform and give form to the society in which it is situated.

In this way the approach addresses what Binder *et al.* (2011) describe as 'a major challenge for design today [which] has to do with what is being designed – not just a "thing" (an object, an "entity of matter") but also a *thing* (a socio-material assembly that deals with matters of concern)'. The approach posits the 'fashion' product, its design process, supply chain, lifecycle and eco-system, as a human-centred, socio-material construction of relational actions, meanings and values. A fashion *thing* that a socially responsive designer can influence, though not dictate, by joining in, in a mindful way.

Consequently, the socially responsive design approach embodies dual purpose in the formation and service of publics through the co-creation of *things*. This is not to describe a social design practice that is in conflict with the market but rather one that seeks to commandeer the making and marketing of products in an attempt to 'fashion' publics and *things*.

Acknowledgements

Much of the content of this chapter draws on collaborative practice and thinking realised with friends and colleagues in Vexed Design Ltd and the Design Against

Crime Research Centre of the University of the Arts London, located at Central Saint Martins (CSM), particularly Joe Hunter and Professor Lorraine Gamman, whom I thank for their generous collaboration. Some of these ideas have been developed through presentation and discussion within the Socially Responsive Design Research Group at CSM, the social innovation track of the AHRC-funded (Arts & Humanities Research Council) FIREup project, and the V&A Design Culture Salon.

Notes

1 The group we knew as the 'Advance Party Network' were referred to as the Advance Party and were linked with the Freedom Network. See http://datacide.c8.com/revolt-of-the-ravers-the-movement-against-the-criminal-justice-act-in-britain-1993-95/ (retrieved 09.07.2014).
2 Police-recorded crime data for London region for 2000 compared to 1998. British Crime Survey for the period 2001/02 compared to 2000/01.
3 A revised edition of the design resource In The Bag is available at www.inthebag.org.uk/whats-in-the-bag/ (retrieved 09.07.2014).
4 'Don't Tempt Me' exhibition, Milan 2001.
5 www.karrysafe.com. Referenced at www.designagainstcrime.com/projects/karrysafe/ (retrieved 09.07.2014).

References

Aldrich, W. (1994) *Metric Pattern Cutting.* London: John Wiley and Sons.

Armitage, R. (2013) *Crime Prevention through Housing Design: Policy and Practice.* Basingstoke, UK: Palgrave Macmillan.

Binder, T., De Michelis, G., Ehn, P., Jacucci, G., Linde, P., Wagner, I. (2011) *Design Things.* Design Thinking, Design Theory. Cambridge, MA: MIT Press.

Björgvinsson, E., Ehn, P., Hillgren, P-A. (2010) Participatory Design and 'Democratizing Innovation'. Proceedings of Participatory Design Conference (PDC), Sydney, Australia, 2010.

Breward, C., Ehrman, E., Evans, C. (2004) *The London Look: Fashion from Street to Catwalk.* London: Yale University Press pp.156–158.

Buchanan, R. (1992) Wicked Problems in Design Thinking. *Design Issues*, 8 (2), 5–21.

Chapman, J. (2005) *Emotionally Durable Design*. London: Earthscan.

Clarke, R. (2008) Situational Crime Prevention, in Wortley, R. and Mazerolle, L. (eds), *Environmental Criminology and Crime Analysis*. Cullompton, UK: Willan.

Crowe, T. (2000) *Crime Prevention through Environmental Design: Applications of Architectural Design and Space Management Concepts*, 2nd edition. Oxford, UK: Butterworth-Heinemann.

Derrida, J. (1983) The Principle of Reason: the University in the Eyes of Its Pupils. *Diacritics*, 13 (3): 2–20.

Dewey, J. (1927) *The Public and Its Problems*. Athens, OH: Swallow Press.

DiSalvo, C. (2009) Design and the Construction of Publics. *Design Issues*, 25 (1), 48–63.

DiSalvo, C., Lodato, T., Fries, L., Schechter, B., Barnwell, T. (eds) (2011) The Collective Articulation of Issues as Design Practice. *CoDesign: International Journal of CoCreation in Design and the Arts*, 7 (3–4), 185–197.

Dunne, A. (1998) *Hertzian Tales: Electronic Products, Aesthetic Experience and Critical Design*. London: Royal College of Art, Computer Related Design Research Publications.

Evans, C. (2003) *Fashion at the Edge: Spectacle, Modernity and Deathliness*. New Haven, CT: Yale University Press pp. 285, 302.

Fischer, G. (2001) Communities of Interest: Learning through the Interaction of Multiple Knowledge Systems. 24th Information Systems Research Seminar in Scandinavia (IRIS24), Bergen, Norway.

Ganman, L., Thorpe, A. (2006) What is Socially Responsive Design? A Theory and Practice Review, in Friedman, K., Love, T., Côrte-Real, E. and Rust, C. (eds) *Design Research Society International Conference Proceedings: Wonderground*. Lisbon, 1–4 November 2006.

Malpass, M. (2013) Between Wit and Reason: Defining Associative, Speculative, and Critical Design in Practice. *Design and Culture*, 5 (3), 333–356.

Morelli, N. (2007) Social Innovation and New Industrial Contexts: Can Designers 'Industrialize' Socially Responsible Solutions? *Design Issues*, 23 (4), 3–21.

Morris, W. (1880) The Beauty of Life, (Lecture), referenced in Waggoner, D. (ed.) (2003) *The Beauty of Life: William Morris and the Art of Design*. London: Thames and Hudson p. 21.

Papanek, V. (1985) *Design for the Real World*, 2nd edition. London: Thames and Hudson.

Papanek, V. (1995) *The Green Imperative: Ecology and Ethics in Design and Architecture*. London: Thames and Hudson.

Rittel, H., Webber, M. (1973) Dilemmas in a General Theory of Planning. *Policy Sciences*, 4 (2), 155–169.

Sennett, R. (2008) *The Craftsman*. London: Allen Lane.

Suchman, L. A. (1987) *Plans and Situated Actions: the Problem of Human–Machine Communication*. Cambridge, UK: Cambridge University Press.

Suchman, L. A., Blomberg, J., Orr, J. E., Trigg, R. (1999) Reconstructing Technologies as Social Practice. *American Behavioral Scientist*, 43 (3), 392–408.

Thorpe, A. and Gamman, L. (2012) Design for Agnostic Space – Reviewing Design Strategies for Conflict Accommodation in 'Wicked' Design Scenarios. Cumulus Helsinki 2012: Northern World Mandate – Towards Open and Participative Cities, Aalto University School of Art and Design, Helsinki, Finland, 24–26 May 2012.

Whiteley, N. (1993) *Design for Society*. London: Reaktion Books p. 110.

Chapter Two

Fashion and textiles design for wellbeing

Value adding through practice-led transdisciplinary design research

Joan Farrer, University of Brighton, UK
Angela Finn, Auckland University of Technology (AUT), New Zealand

Design researchers from many areas are beginning to explore a key question in the twenty-first century in order to contribute towards a vision and reason for their disciplines: can products be designed to have added value to the consumer and at the same time contribute to improved outcomes for the health and wellbeing of the user? Can society be improved by changing the design of products around us? (Goulev and Farrer 2013). This chapter provides an overview of some design and technological developments from the global fashion and textiles industry, endorsing a model where designers and technicians use their transferable skills to create products for wellbeing rather than desire. The opportunities offered by research in the area of smart textiles for improved health and wellbeing are discussed in relation to three different research projects in the first part of the chapter. The second part of this chapter explores low cost, low tech or 'dumb' approaches, using methods such as requirement analysis and user-centred design, which have offered an alternative to expensive high tech, smart materials and pharmaceutical applications in researching the prevention of skin cancer. The idea of value adding is applied at the design stage and is recognised in the research process and in the marketplace. The aim is to explore how practice-led research in fashion and textiles, as a part of a transdisciplinary research framework, can contribute to practical solutions for key problems faced by researchers in the fields of health and wellbeing. The proposition is that collaboration between practitioners in fashion and textiles (Arts) and scientific researchers (STEM science, technology, engineering and maths) in the field of medical research, including health and wellbeing for example, offers a paradigm shift for the discipline and could facilitate the best opportunities for successful research and development outcomes in addressing serious health issues.

Background

Textiles is one of the oldest and most important disciplines. The word 'textile' comes from the Latin root *textillis*, meaning woven.

> Many phrases in the English language have come from this ancient industry, where cloth remnants have been found from 36,000BP (before present) and fashion and textiles meanings are subliminally embedded into our culture. Phrases like 'after a fashion' meaning to follow a style or behaviour, 'fabric of society', 'folded into', 'text' from textile, 'tailor-made', customized, a 'thread of conversation', the list of 'material' is substantial.
>
> (Farrer 2011: 22)

Textiles have protected us from the elements and have clothed us for modesty. Fabrics have protected our human skins from damage, replacing fur and leather as clothing. Textiles were used early for wellbeing in northern Europe and this has been well documented since the fifteenth and sixteenth centuries. Since Egyptian times, fabrics have been used for medical applications including bandages, and woven flax used to wrap the mummified bodies of royalty (Figure 2.1). Sometimes these ancient cloths incorporated natural products such as flax or honey to aid healing. It could be argued that they were early *smart* textiles; however in general these textiles were 'dumb'.

It was with the advent of synthetic fibres and textile engineering, at the end of the nineteenth century, that smart applications began to be seen. Today contemporary fabrics are used to carry medicine and to restrict and control pressure on limbs; they are even combined internally in the body to create improvements. Examples of emerging developments in smart textiles, for applications in the medical sector, include shape memory alloy and fully fashioned knitted textile polyamides for surgical applications for ostomy procedures.

Smart materials

Smart materials in the form of responsive and adaptive fibres and fabrics combined with electro-active devices and ICT are increasingly shaping many aspects of

Figure 2.1: Ancient Egyptian bandages from the 26th Dynasty.

society, and have been embraced by the leisure industry and interactive consumer; however, these products are ever more visible in healthcare. Combinations of biocompatible delivery devices with bio-sensing elements can create, analyse, sense and actuate early warning and monitoring systems which can be linked to data logging and patient records via intelligent networks. Patient sympathetic, 'smart' fashion/textiles applications based on interdisciplinary expertise utilising textiles design and technology is an emerging Research and Development field.

Contemporary 'smart' fashion and textiles have various functions which include *sensing*, *actuating*, *powering*, *generating*, *storing*, *communicating*, *data processing* and *connecting*. However, traditional or 'dumb' textiles also have the power to *sense* conditions and respond to changes in these conditions. For example, the cellulose structure of cotton enables it to cool the skin in heat. When changes in the environment are felt, wool *actuates* a wicking effect and will pull moisture away from the skin to keep it dry. Flax will react to temperature and will absorb moisture four times more successfully than cotton; it can also release oils that act as an anti-bacterial agent. *Powering* is found in early man-made fabrics which conduct static electricity. *Communicating* happens in dumb cloth, also through the power of touch. *Data processing*, it could be argued, is created by visual stimuli. *Connecting* occurs between people through emotion and a desire for display using clothing.

One of the newest areas in fashion and textile development is the area of smart and interactive textiles. This is vanguard research where computer technology and electrical interactivity are combined with fashion and textiles; it is still in its infancy and the hoped-for outcomes are not yet realised as interdisciplinary developments. The technology is developing at a rapid rate and has the potential to affect many fields, including medical applications. Schwarz *et al.* suggest:

> the convergence of textiles and electronics can be exemplarily pointed out for their development of smart material, which is capable of accomplishing a wide spectrum of functions found in rigid and inflexible electronics today. Smart textiles could serve as a means to increase the well-being of society and they might lead to important savings on the health budget.
>
> (2010: 101)

With smart fibres and textiles it is possible for micro-electronics to be integrated into garments for personal customisation and wellbeing. The first evidence of electronics being integrated into fabric was in 1921, in the form of an electric blanket developed for sanatorium patients with tuberculosis (Bellis n.d.). This was a simple resistive heating coil sandwiched between two fabrics and was developed so that the tuberculosis patients could sit outside in the fresh air and remain warm. Today electronic textiles allow the community of users to interact seamlessly with their environment via sophisticated multimedia with WiFi technology, RFID (radio frequency identification) and microcomputers creating smart products which are sensitive to people's needs.

Wearable electronics have until now in fact been 'portable' rather than 'wearable' and have used bolt-on technology, such as electrical components that run off large heavy batteries, strapped to the body. The challenge now is to achieve discreet wearable electronics which act ubiquitously within the fabric and perform invisibly. For instance, now that power sources are becoming more sophisticated, solar batteries are reducing in size and it is becoming more feasible to incorporate the technology and create a wearable device. Early workers in this area focused on miniaturisation of computing technologies but engineers in the electronics field were not aware of the dynamics of fabric or garment design and the issues of performance, motion and desire. Since researchers from these fields have been working collaboratively with design experts they have been able to form tacit understandings of emotional design – which brings to the product the importance of function in combination with form, and links desire to practical solutions. Early developers in this field, such as Philips Electronics Ltd and *SOFT*switch Ltd (Rodie 2004), and research projects such as MIT's 'Visions of the Future' (Fibretronic Ltd n.d.) and 'Design for Life' (Brunel University 2013) use experimental embroidered conductive thread, felted fabric and knitted and woven cloths containing elementary pressure sensors.

This is a key function of wearable technology. Textiles which allow conductivity, audio, data and power to be moved around a garment have mindboggling applications as yet undiscovered. The wearer no longer needs to be connected to a permanent power supply or attached to electrical cables. This is particularly useful in medical applications. Getting power into and out of a fabric, without breaking the circuit, is a challenge. Conductivity can be activated using wire, conductive printing inks, a conductive layer such as foam padding or a fabric with a metal coated surface. Fabrics which are treated or blended with conductive materials such as nickel, carbon, steel or silver can create pathways to carry electronic information in the fabrics and clothing. Another method is to use conductive inks, which can be screened directly on to the fabric to operate as switches or pressure pads for the activation of printed circuits; in this way a telephone control panel, for example, can be created on a garment. Several companies are developing solutions for medical monitoring where a patient or user, such as a 'first responder', can communicate with a doctor or manager to monitor a person's heart or respiratory rate or rhythm, and temperature. These vital signs monitoring systems can include global positioning systems (GPS) for ease, pinpointing the location in a building on fire or on a battlefield, for instance. One company active in this field is Zephyr Technologies Ltd in New Zealand (Science Learning Hub 2013).

Solar power is one good way of generating energy, through fibres woven into fabric and activated by sunlight. These solar fabrics are less sophisticated and productive than crystalline solar cells, which are now being miniaturised and made more flexible, and can therefore be used much more easily as electrical generators for the body. Another method of generating power is the human battery, which allows heat generated by the wearer to be gathered to supply power, giving it an unlimited lifespan. Energy produced by motion is also under development and was first pioneered in the area of wrist watches with kinetic motion. The possible applications for integrated electrical communication are enormous, particularly in the fields of entertainment, toys and fashion – where these blue sky applications are often first adapted. However, it is in the fields of wellbeing, physical disability, the ageing population and the medical sector that the real smart textiles applications are still to be developed.

The main stumbling block to this development is the idea of transdisciplinarity where numerous fields must work together autonomously to produce one invention. Large investments in the field of smart and interactive textiles have been made in research and development at Massachusetts Institute of Technology (MIT) in the USA. They have developed research projects using electrical and conductive fibres. For instance, these fibres are connected to sensors which can transmit data about the speed or direction of a bullet as it strikes the wearer. The sensor can then transmit this data to a medical unit where staff can use it to deliver care quickly and effectively to the patient on the battlefield. Another smart application in the field is optical camouflage; data can be collected and then linked to fibre optic technology. A background image can be projected on to a body and the garments become transparent as they blend into the surroundings. For the purposes of defence, new liquid crystal electro-chromic technologies electrically alter molecules to detect a soldier's background environment and change colour and pattern in the fabric accordingly, negating the need for different uniforms.

It was Philips Ltd in 1995 who first coined the phrase *wearable electronics* (Hibbert 2001: 106). Philips created a unique team of textile designers, electronic engineers, garment designers and computing experts to work on blue sky applications for clients such as Nike and Levi Strauss. Here the technology was clunky and bolt-on. Today the use of radio frequency identification (RFID) technology (commonly known as 'tagging') is widely used and sophisticated. Tags can be implanted into nano-polymers to track and trace people around the globe. In a modern hospital textiles appear in many applications: in implants to replace tendons; tissue engineering for burns reconstruction; and hygiene and healthcare products such as bedding and protective covers. Protection in bandages for wounds and operating room gowns or as packaging for surgical implements and last but not least for clinician's uniforms. Medical textiles are divided into three types identified by Slater (2003:194) as 'those external to the body or intended to be transplanted into it, those in the healthcare field and those strictly concerned with hygiene'.

Medical clothing and textiles include a wide variety of fabrics, from those designed to protect from the transfer of micro-organisms through to specific engineering and performance fabrics that are resistant to liquid, yet have good moisture and vapour permeability, to allow patient comfort to be maintained. Internal uses of textiles include grafts and implants (see Ramakrishna 2001). Textiles with multi-component layers are used in dialysis treatment and can be 'tuned' for use as artificial blood vessels. Embroidery techniques have been used for testing implants for disc repair in the shoulder or neck. Dyer (2011) has developed shape memory alloy in woven textiles for arterial stents which expand to a pre-programmed body temperature. New fabrics developed for abdominal fissures, aneurysms and ruptures use design engineering in woven or warp knitted fabric with directional stretch to mimic muscle performance. These textiles for internal use are sometimes made from bioresorbable fibres (where tissue can bond with the textile) and are treated with biocompatible film that can be implanted to aid the regeneration of the body after damage or are used in the controlled release of a drug. Other textile applications in medicine include a novel dressing (to treat burns, for example) that can, over a predetermined period, provide sustained release of anti-microbial compounds, accelerating the growth of new skin while preventing bacterial entry. Mast Carbon® have developed an ultra filter made from woven and non-woven material, devised to provide improved filtration for liquids or gas molecules through engineered carbon fibre design. It features holes of specific sizes, and permeability can be modified to let through molecules of a certain size; it can be used for face masks and wound dressings.

'Signalling' textiles can play a part in early warning systems where thermo-chromic dyes are important. Thermo-chromic inks are intelligent materials capable of responding to their environment. They can be made as semiconductor materials, using liquid crystal compounds, which can respond to room temperature by changing colour depending on a number of different predetermined temperatures. Also in this category are reflective textiles, used in photonic fabrics; a single fibre can be tuned to reflect light at different wavelengths to create a kind of optical barcode, which can be woven into fabric to identify the wearer. These fibres can also be designed to reflect thermal radiation over various ranges. Signalling textiles can include electroluminescence, whereby phosphate powder is encased in a flat polyester film. An electric current excites the phosphorus molecules to emit a gentle light in a consistent and uniform fashion. Electroluminescence was first developed in 1936 and has been used in watch faces, for example. Also included in the 'signalling' category are textiles using fibre optics, which can transmit information about colour, light or even pattern through the fibre. However, these are technologies without specific applications.

Textiles can have intelligent protective systems where the fabric can protect against skin cancer or premature ageing of the skin; these are key concerns in parts of the world where protection from harmful UVB rays (ultraviolet radiation), which cause acute sunburn, is in development. In general, the darker the colour of the fabric, the higher the sun protection factor rating. Fabrics with a high UPF (Ultraviolet Protection Factor) sunscreen rating absorb UV rays, rather than blocking them; polyester and certain polyamides are particularly good at absorbing dangerous rays. The inclusion of ceramic molecules in a synthetic fibre or surface coating can deflect harmful rays. This type of fabric can withstand wash and wear processes and remain effective. Tighter and denser weaves give increased protection, whereas standard cotton stretch weaves allow harmful rays through the cloth when the cloth is extended.

Designing solutions to research problems

Smart textiles offer high tech solutions for improved health and wellbeing but the science alone is not enough. The role of the designer is significant as a means of connecting the product with the consumer. Research can benefit from a transdisciplinary approach that combines practice-led design research with engineering and scientific research methods. One such case is the 'Scrap the Cap' design project (see Figure 2.3) that was developed around the prevention of serious skin cancer, where the majority of research investment has been focused on scientific research and educational awareness campaigns. Sun protection factors (SPF) were first established in Australia and New Zealand; however melanoma is increasing despite the millions of dollars that are being spent on SPF creams each year. The research project, which began as a collaboration between Cancer Society Auckland (CSA) and Auckland University of Technology (AUT) in early 2007, demonstrates the advantages of the methods of design practice in offering an alternative solution to the problem of preventing serious skin cancer within a specific target age group (18–24-year-olds) in New Zealand. In adolescence and young adulthood our bodies are exposed to 80 per cent of the total harmful radiation that we will encounter during our lifespan. While millions have been invested in possible scientific methods of skin cancer prevention, in drug and medical research, the existing approaches have not been effective within this particular age group, where instances of melanoma are showing no sign of decreasing. There is a gap in knowledge around effective interventions for what remains a serious health issue.

A promising approach to the prevention of skin cancer has been an on-going campaign known as 'Slip! Slop! Slap!' started in Australia in 1980. The programme was instigated to encourage Australians to reduce the risk of skin cancer (or 'sun cancer'), which was recognised as becoming a very serious health issue. The current SunSmart™ programme, which raises awareness of 'sun smart' behaviours alongside a schools accreditation programme, has been able to demonstrate some success in contributing to reducing rates of skin cancer (Montague *et al.* 2001). A large focus has been to encourage school age students to avoid being out in the sun during the most damaging times of day (10 a.m. to 3 p.m.) and to wear appropriate clothing – a protective hat and a shirt with sleeves – when they are outside during school hours. From its early beginnings as a jingle encouraging viewers to 'Slip on a shirt, slop on sunscreen and slap on a hat', sung by the cartoon character Sid Seagull, developments in research around sun protection have shown that there are different levels of protection offered by different hat designs. Cancer Society Auckland, through its association with The Australian Cancer Society (now The Cancer Council Australia), has access to the results of scientific tests performed on existing hat products within the marketplace. The aim was to determine which styles provided the most protection from the harmful effects of the sun and resulted in 'the dimensions contained in a "magic" formula' (Farrer and Finn 2010: 682): the ideal specifications for a SunSmart™ hat.

The results indicated that three particular styles, the Bucket Hat (Figure 2.2), the Legionnaire's Hat and the Broad-Brimmed Hat, offered the best case scenario for providing optimal sun protection. The recommendation of these designs worked well within the SunSmart™ School programmes (Cancer Society of New Zealand 2013) aimed at primary school students, but a problem was emerging in those aged between 18 and 24 years. This is an age group where the fashion is to wear cotton T-Shirts and shorts suited to an outdoorsy lifestyle, and teenage boys going *without* a shirt is a particular issue. Clearly, fashion and peer pressure play some role in labelling certain styles 'uncool' and therefore, without any formal governance, the intended benefits of the most protective hats were not achieved. In other words, the scientific testing did not consider that the target group least likely to protect themselves against the risks of skin cancer was being influenced by current fashion in making a decision on what would otherwise be a clear choice for future health and wellbeing. The

6 cm

Figure 2.2: Bucket Hat.
Source: Cancer Society of New Zealand 2007.

project challenged young designers, from a similar age demographic, to develop designs that would have potential appeal to the target group.

The hat project, dubbed 'Scrap the Cap' in reference to the preferred style of hat worn by young people in New Zealand, began with the clear remit of creating a more desirable hat design that would appeal to this target group but would also offer better sun protection. The project was run with a group of student designers from the undergraduate fashion programme at AUT University in Auckland, New Zealand. The focus of the project was structured within the parameters of a design brief, formulated as a competition, sponsored by Cancer Society Auckland (see Figure 2.3). The research question was: Is it possible to develop a prototype hat design which 18–24-year-olds would want to wear, and which would also provide adequate protection from the sun? And could scientific specifications be satisfied and incorporated into such a fashion accessory? A design practice methodology was used to frame the study and included the steps of prototyping (sketching, pattern making and sampling) to respond to the research question. The design process, from requirements analysis to experimental concept and prototype development, was used to formulate the most elegant design solution within the constraints of the findings of the scientific tests conducted by Cancer Society Auckland. The aim was to develop a prototype product, with the winner of the

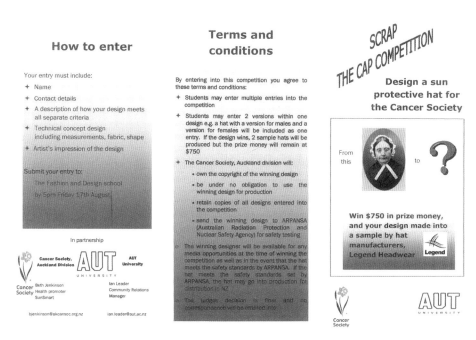

Figure 2.3: Scrap the Cap competition design brief.
Source: AUT and Cancer Society of New Zealand Auckland Division Inc. 2007.

design competition working with a local hat producer to develop a sample hat that could be tested by the ARPANSA (Australian Radiation Protection and Nuclear Safety Agency) and compared to the three designs recommended at the time by the Cancer Society in Australia and New Zealand. This testing would provide a quantitative measure of the effectiveness of the protection offered by the prototype through a series of staged tests.

In terms of determining the qualitative measure of 'cool' or 'not cool' the winning design was chosen by members of the target age group who voted on the design layouts from five finalists that were printed in *Debate* magazine (AuSM 2013), the magazine of AUT University's student union movement (AuSM). The hat design that was awarded the most votes was created by the then 22-year-old design student Priyanka Pierra (Figure 2.4). The design was an interpretation of the traditional legionnaire's hat with a twist, offered by the tweaking of fabrication and colour, to bring the function of the original design into the realm of a fashion object. The final testing at the Australian Radiation Protection and Nuclear Safety Agency[1] revealed that the designer hat also out-performed the traditional

Figure 2.4: Design layout of winning hat design by Priyanka Pierra (2007).

legionnaire's hat that was commercially available (Figure 2.5). This was as a result of the fabric used and the slight variation in the size and fit of the distinctive back and side flaps of the new design. The combination of materiality and relationship to the body are key aspects of fashion research in creating desire where none exists. This has been discussed elsewhere, in terms of fashion encouraging bad behaviours such as over-production and over-consumption, but the use of fashion as a vehicle for change in terms of consumer behaviour is often overlooked. In this case, the knowledge of a student designer is able to transport a clunky, scientific, functional object – that was limited in its effectiveness due to its lack of use within a specific target age demographic – into one that has the opportunity to reach its full potential as a barrier-type solution to the prevention of serious skin cancer.

Conclusion

Fashion and textiles design has much to answer for in contributing to the problems of unsustainable practices in design, production and waste on a global scale. However,

Figure 2.5: Controlled testing at ARPANSA (2008).

design-led research within this field also has great potential to contribute to practical solutions. This chapter has discussed a series of developments in the area of smart textiles which provide enormous opportunity for design practitioners to exploit the concept of value adding through technological garment and textiles applications and enhancement for health and wellbeing. The case study presented encourages the use of design as a practice-led methodology that offers equally viable, inexpensive, low tech solutions to what are serious research problems. The method has these advantages: it offers the potential of multiple viable solutions for relatively minimal investment, and the knowledge required to connect consumer behaviour with actions likely to promote the prevention of serious health issues. In this case, fashion design practice and the methods of the design process provided an alternative approach to the problem of developing improved practices in the field of protective clothing to prevent skin cancer. In turn, the practice-led research project came up with a potential solution to the low use of protective hats within the 18–24-year-old age group, the group most likely to do nothing to protect themselves against the risk of developing serious skin cancer. The skill set involved in working with a narrow and specific target market, an essential element for successful professional practice in design, can be applied to a research problem such as this. The low cost of prototyping, compared to the millions of dollars spent on funding drug and chemical solutions, could allow the development of a greater number of possible alternative options for fashion and wellbeing to be combined into elegant solutions that are universal and almost as *seamless* as those offered by the high tech smart textiles solutions. This particular research problem is ideally suited to a research solution involving fashion design practice, but there are many problems where solutions rely on engaging user behaviours, and practice-led research paradigms, such as design, can make a significant contribution. The challenge is to combine low tech research methods and practice with emerging technologies to ensure optimal solutions, particularly when dealing with critical research problems surrounding health and wellbeing.

Note

1 www.arpansa.gov.au (accessed 4 July 2014).

References

Auckland Student Movement (AuSM). 2013. *Debate* magazine [online]. Auckland, New Zealand: AuSM (Auckland Student Movement). Available: www.ausm. org.nz/?page=debate (accessed 2 December 2013).

Auckland University of Technology (AUT) and Cancer Society Auckland (CSA). 2007. Scrap the Cap competition [flyer]. Auckland, New Zealand: Cancer Society of New Zealand.

Australian Radiation Protection and Nuclear Safety Authority (ARPANSA). 2008. *Hat testing for the Scrap the Cap prototype* [digital photograph]. Sydney: ARPANSA.

Bellis, M. n.d. History of the electric blanket [online]. Available: http://inventors. about.com/od/estartinventions/a/ElectricBlanket.htm (accessed 2 December 2013).

Brunel University. 2013. School of Engineering and Design, Design Research [online]. Available: www.brunel.ac.uk/sed/design/research (accessed 2 December 2013).

Cancer Society of New Zealand. 2007. Hats: protecting your head, neck and face. [Information sheet]. Auckland, New Zealand: Cancer Society of New Zealand.

Cancer Society of New Zealand. 2013. SunSmart schools programme [online]. Wellington, New Zealand: Cancer Society of New Zealand. Available: www. sunsmartschools.co.nz/schools/accreditation (accessed 2 December 2013).

Dyer, P. 2011. *Dynamic control of active textiles: the integration of nickel-titanium shape memory alloys and the manipulation of woven structures*. PhD thesis. Brighton, UK: University of Brighton.

Farrer, J. 2011. Remediation: discussing fashion textiles sustainability. In: Gwilt, A. and Rissanen, T. (eds) *Shaping sustainable fashion: changing the way we make and use clothes*. London: Earthscan.

Farrer, J. and Finn, A. 2010. The power of a single prototype: sustainable fashion textile design and the prevention of carcinogenic melanoma. In: Bartolo, P. *et al.* (eds) *Innovative developments in design and manufacturing: Proceedings of the 4th International Conference on Advanced Research in Virtual and Rapid Prototyping, Leiria, Portugal.* Boca Raton, FL; London: Taylor & Francis.

Fibretronic Ltd. n.d. Wearables reaches its 10th year: Part 1: the early pioneers. Available: http://fibretronic.com/news/Wearables%20Review (accessed 15 April 2014).

Goulev, P. and Farrer, J. 2013. Interactive design activism. *Awareness* magazine [online]. Available: www.awareness-mag.eu/view.php?source=004899-2013-05-24 (accessed 6 December 2013).

Hibbert, R. 2001. *Textile innovation: traditional, modern and smart textiles.* London: Line Publishing.

Montague, M., Borland, R. and Sinclair, C. 2001. Slip! Slop! Slap! and SunSmart, 1980–2000: skin cancer control and 20 years of population-based campaigning. *Health Education & Behavior*, 28(3), 290–305.

Pierra, P. 2007. *Priyanka Pierra: Scrap the Cap competition entry.* [Design layout]. Auckland, New Zealand: AUT University.

Ramakrishna, S. 2001. Textile scaffolds in tissue engineering. In: Tao, X. (ed.) *Smart fibres, fabrics and clothing.* Cambridge, UK: Woodhead Publishing.

Rodie, J. B. 2004. Textile sensitivity. *Textile World*, 154(6), 82. Available: www.textileworld.com/Issues/2004/June/Quality_Fabric_Of_The_Month/Textile_Sensitivity (accessed 15 April 2014).

Schwarz, A., Van Langenhove, L., Guermonprez, P. and Deguillemont, D. 2010. A roadmap on smart textiles. *Textile Progress*, 42(2), 99–180.

Science Learning Hub. 2013. *Innovations – Zephyr Technology* [online]. Hamilton, New Zealand: University of Waikato. Available: www.sciencelearn.org.nz/Science-Stories/TVNZ-Innovation-Stories/Sci-Media/Video/Innovations-Zephyr-Technology (accessed 2 December 2013).

Slater, K. 2003. *Environmental impact of textiles: production, processes and protection.* Cambridge, UK: Woodhead Publishing.

Chapter Three

Design for ageing well

Jane McCann, University of South Wales, UK

Introduction

This chapter discusses fashion design that has the potential to enrich our social, environmental and cultural lives. In particular it looks at functional clothing, for the rapidly growing active ageing population, that enables wearers to engage in healthy exercise. It discusses how older wearers may benefit from the comfort attributes of easy care fabrics and the ergonomic cut of the functional sports clothing 'layering system'. It looks at how real user design requirements may be identified and addressed through adopting a collaborative design approach. It reports on cross-disciplinary research in a case study concerned with the application of smart textiles and wearable electronics in clothing for walking. It stresses the importance of the role of designers in acting 'as connectors and facilitators, as quality producers, as visualizers and visionaries, as future builders (or co-producers)', as promoters of new business models and as catalysers of change. (Fuad-Luke 2009).

Preparing for demographic change

The 50-plus community is rapidly growing and will soon represent the 'new consumer majority' but, to date, there remains within the fashion business a poor image of ageing. Demographic change is a major challenge to the design profession – and the business community, which commissions it (Economist 2002). 'Baby Boomers', the 'Third Age' and, in terms of academic research, the 'Active Ageing' have clothing design needs that are not being addressed by current, transient, mainstream fashion. This group has enjoyed being stylish since being the centre of attention in the 'swinging Sixties'. In theory they have disposable income but they are dissatisfied with what is currently available in the retail environment, for a variety of reasons (McCann 2013).

There are 10.3 million people in the UK aged 65 and over, representing an 80 per cent increase over six decades from 1951. The number of people aged 65 and over is projected to increase 23 per cent, from 10.3 million in 2010 to 12.7 million in 2018, with growth in this age group projected to continue and the 65-plus population expected to reach 16.9 million by 2035. Globally, the number of people aged 60 and over will nearly triple, increasing from 894 million in 2010 to 2.43 billion in 2050 (Rutherford 2012). Rapidly ageing populations, and growing numbers of people with disabilities, are having a profound effect on new product and service development. The need for a more socially inclusive approach to designing is rising up the business agenda. Design development to include the needs of marginalised groups is regarded as not just socially desirable but a commercial opportunity, since 'Over the past two decades, consumption by the over-50s in Europe has increased three times as fast as that by the rest of the population' (Economist 2002).

New ways to think about fashion design

The active ageing

Many baby boomers who may have had an earlier obsession with physical appearance are undergoing a 'change of attitude in ways quite normal for people in mid-life' and 'are quite far ahead on the road to the higher levels of humanness that leads to dramatic changes in buying behaviour' (Wolfe and Snyder 2003). 'Designer labels are about making social statements, and as people move into and through the second half of life, interest in designer labels falls off because they are not as compelled to make social statements by their brand choices' (ibid.). The purchasing behaviour of older consumers may be related more to health, independence and self-sufficiency than to other factors normally considered in market segmentation (Metz and Underwood 2005). Perhaps mature customers are forced into more rational purchase behaviour because brands that could be aspirational for this segment do not (yet) exist (ibid.).

Particular aspects of physical performance that decline with age include mobility, dexterity and the ability to reach and stretch (Metz and Underwood 2005). These changes are not necessarily pathological but are natural patterns of change associated with ageing. Requirements for functional clothing for those with loss of strength, for instance, will affect the design of fastenings and packaging. Dressing and undressing will demand greater ease of movement. Older people are less tolerant of extremes in temperature. Changes in posture, shape and measurement proportions within the body will affect the hang or balance of the cut, fit and comfort of the clothing; changes in visual acuity, meanwhile, demand special consideration in choosing font and font size, surfaces, colour, degree of glare, back lighting, angle of light, and so on (Wolfe and Snyder 2003). Clothing and product designers need to take these changes into account in the design of wearable technology user-interfaces (McCann 2012).

The image of ageing

> Images of ageing have a great influence on both the realization of development potentials in old age and on dealing with the restrictions of old age. The future of old age thus depends to a large degree on images of ageing. Yet the images of ageing that dominate our society often do not do justice to the diversity of old age.
>
> (German Federal Ministry for Family Affairs 2011)

Not all women as they get older relish the prospect of dressing in baggy cardigans, comfort waistbands and fluffy slippers. It's true, though, that comfort does become more of a consideration. What is surprising, despite all we hear about the West's ageing baby-boomer population bulge, is how poorly served older women still feel by the fashion industry (Willis 2013).

> 'Fashion is pleasant until the age of 60,' writes an 84-year-old former architect, 'after that we are forgotten.' And stereotypes prevail: the industry, says a 78-year-old retired solicitor, 'should accept that women over 60 don't all want to dress in black bombazine'. Whatever the effects and restrictions that come with it, age doesn't necessarily wither our pride in our appearance. Perhaps when today's young designers get their bus passes, they will at last address this. Our challenge to them? Don't wait that long.
>
> (ibid.)

Dame Vivienne Westwood has also criticised the rise of 'disposable fashion' and warned that it makes us all look the same and that only 70-year-old women display any sense of style these days. She suggests that women of her age are better used to choosing key pieces suited to individual style (Thomas 2012). Journalist Katharine Whitehorn states that 'it's easy for young people to be trendy, but the fashion fraternity has got it all wrong when it comes to older women' (Whitehorn 2012). She observes that the fashion industry has been prone to such portrayals as the following: 'bone thin models with long white hair who looked as if they'd been starving on a desert island for two years paraded before the real-life mature women watching, who wore styles that suited their varying shapes.' In terms of image, 'older women are more confident in many ways, but this is usually tempered by a sensible desire to conceal the bits that are no longer perfect'. Whitehorn has 'long wished the fashion fraternity would visit such gatherings of real older women to see what they actually wear' (ibid.).

The concept of 'age-affirmative branding celebrates age and uses it as a central theme in developing a brand personality' (Moody and Sood 2010). Age-affirmative brands promise a positive benefit linked to age. They do not ignore or deny age but instead focus on elements we can celebrate and affirm, conveying a message of hope and positive ageing. 'The key success factor is to embrace the benefits of ageing without stereotyping seniors. In other words, the branding program needs to understand and perhaps celebrate the lifestyle of the older consumer' (ibid.). One of the most remarkable examples of a different type of age-affirmative branding was the Dove campaign 'Pro-Age', which focused on a line of personal care products and launched the study 'Beauty Comes of Age' (2007). The Dove campaign, more broadly, 'was a vehicle for age resistance, a challenge to prevailing ageist attitudes in society, and an effort to replace denial and avoidance with age-affirmative branding' (ibid.).

> Baby boomers were the original teenagers, which is why the two groups may have similar values, suggests a study by The Sound Research, shown exclusively to *Marketing Week*. Before the boomer generation reached their teens in the Fifties, the concept of 'teenagers' didn't exist. Boomers may now be middle aged, or even approaching retirement, but as the first teenagers, they do not consider themselves old.
>
> (Handley 2011)

Size and shape

Clothing brands tend to have individual approaches to determining garment sizing, which causes considerable confusion among the end-users. This is both in terms of measurement and in the naming of sizes, exacerbated by vanity sizing, calculated to flatter you into buying because you can fit into a smaller-than-usual size. Willis reports, 'As a 49-year-old florist from Ireland put it: "I used to be a size 12 and now I'm a size 10, but I haven't got any thinner." We want clothes to flatter our bodies, not our minds' (Willis 2013). Older consumers do not understand how sizing can differ so much, even within ranges produced by one brand (McCann 2013). They wonder why we cannot have a universal sizing system, particularly in the era of Internet shopping. In theory there is a European standard for labelling clothes sizes, EN 13402, although this has not had an obvious impact on user retail experience.

Willis says:

> Above all we would like our clothes to fit us. We want more petite and tall sizes; we want half sizes, in clothes and in shoes; we want legs and sleeves in several lengths; we want in-house alteration. ... The market needs 'a middle way between couture and off-the-peg, a bit of pin and tuck' ... A lot of women said they pay to have their clothes altered, adding to the price-tag; and many dream of having someone to alter their clothes and make them fit properly.
>
> (2013)

Willis reports that 'it's common for women to have at least three different sizes in their cupboards; one of our respondents pointed out that she "owns and wear[s] garments ranging from size 10 to XL"' (2013). She says:

> Women want to find brands that 'provide interesting quirky variations on classic themes'; brands that make clothes that fit us: each of us, not Mrs Average, whoever she is. We don't want to waste time every season working out which label fits us this time.
>
> (ibid.)

User dissatisfaction with poor fit is a major cause of waste within the garment industry. 'The fashion industry is enormously clever but not particularly smart. It has a short-term focus on immediate payoff, on novelty, and innovation but really does not pay attention in a smart way to its own long-term needs' (Coates 2005). The situation is perhaps most dramatic in women's clothing, but it has also affected men with the movement towards small, medium and large. 'What one finds is that men's clothes are increasingly designed to fit no known primate. The industry, having distorted all sizes, has created an obstacle to their own success in marketing clothes through catalogs and on the Internet' (ibid.). Coates predicted that bespoke clothing would become more and more routine and popular.

> Digital photography to collect size data from the individual will allow merchants to build a complete archive of clothes styles, sizes, and so on for each customer. Factory machinery will create a garment that will have a 98 percent correct fit with wrap-up changes made by a human tailor. The implications of this are that once one has gotten information into the database, no more visits to the department store or to the clothing store will be needed.
>
> (ibid.)

Until the wearer changed shape or changed in weight, everything would be handled electronically through the Internet (Coates 2005). National anthropometric studies such as SizeUK,[1] SizeUSA and SizeGermany have now taken place, with others planned.

More responsible/sustainable processes

User-led design

Sanders and Stappers (2008) state that 'The evolution in design research from a user-centred approach to co-designing is changing the roles of the designer, the researcher and the person formerly known as the "user".' They confirm that, in their view, the role of designers, as researchers, remains key 'to lead people in the visual expression of their creativity, guide those who wish to adapt "products" and concepts and support people in contributing to the practical development level of creativity'. Designers, say Sanders and Stappers,

> play a role on the co-designing teams because they provide expert knowledge that the other stakeholders do not have. Designers professionally keep track of

existing, new and emerging technologies, and have an overview of production processes and business contexts. This knowledge will still be relevant throughout the design development process.

(ibid.)

Inclusive design is neither a new genre of design, nor a separate specialism. It is a general approach to designing in which designers ensure that their products and services address the needs of the widest possible audience, irrespective of age or ability. Two major trends have driven the growth of Inclusive Design (also known as Design for All, and as Universal Design in the USA): population ageing and the growing movement to integrate disabled people into mainstream society (Design Council n.d.). When designing for a different age range, the designers need to be attuned to the aesthetic and aspirational values of the users, given that:

Each generation will have developed different sets of technological skills, knowledge and experience. … What users want from products will be derived from their knowledge of existing and previous products. However, when considering the design of a radical new technology, the usefulness of the feedback will potentially be restricted by the ability of the participants to understand its potential. This is true for both the mainstream market and the 'special needs' market.

(Cambridge Engineering Design Centre 2005)

Product acceptability

Inclusive, user-led design approaches and accessibility have been commonplace in product design and in the area of computer technology user-interfaces but have been given little consideration in clothing design. The Engineering Design Centre (EDC) in Cambridge proposes that, to be acceptable, a product must be both socially and practically acceptable. Social acceptability is what most product designers try to achieve with their products. As such, inclusive design does not require the application of new skills or techniques but requires the designer to modify his or her perception of what the user really wants. Obtaining and interpreting those requirements needs specialised approaches. In identifying the user wants and aspirations, the EDC process addresses the following issues:

- Does the product look nice?
- Do I trust this product?
- Does this product stigmatise me in any way?
- Do I want this product?
- Is this product 'cool'?

Having considered designing for the goal of social acceptability, the next step is to consider practical acceptability; this is divided into:

- cost
- compatibility
- reliability
- usefulness: subdivided into utility and usability.

Utility is described as the provision of the necessary functionality by the product or service to perform the desired task, while *usability* is defined as including ease of learning, efficiency of use, ease of remembering and low (user) error rates (Cambridge Engineering Design Centre 2005). Little inclusive design work has been done to date on functional clothing.

Identification of design requirements for functional clothing

The author has developed a design process, specific to functional clothing design, that has helped to guide the design for ageing research. Her identification of end-user design requirements (Figure 3.1) balances form with function, represented as a tree of topics to provide design guidance (McCann 1999, 2009).

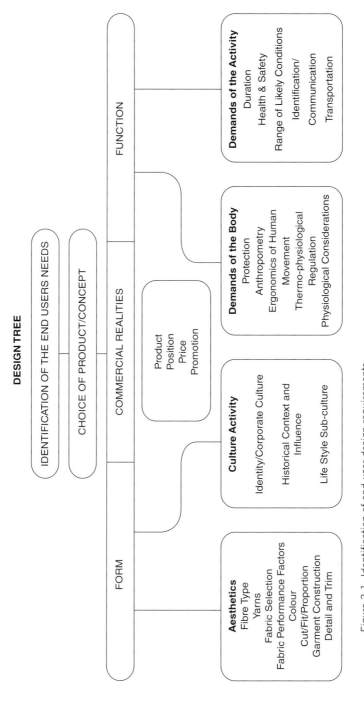

Figure 3.1: Identification of end-user design requirements.

Source: Adapted from McCann 1999. Diagram by David Bryson.

Case study: a co-design approach to design for ageing well

Introducing the project

The 'Design for Ageing Well' collaborative research project, funded by the joint UK Research Councils under the New Dynamics of Ageing programme (NDA),[2] provides a case study. This research demonstrates how clothing design can positively contribute to addressing problems associated with everyday life that are normally unfamiliar to mainstream fashion and educational design studies. In particular it looks at the application of smart textiles and wearable electronics in functional clothing for the active ageing. In adopting the comfort attributes of lightweight, breathable and protective materials, the aim has been to create a stylish clothing layering system, with integrated technology, that has the potential to promote independence, social engagement (with the focus on healthy exercise) and, in particular, walking.

A collaborative network brought together cross-disciplinary academic researchers from across five universities, merging the topics of design, public involvement in care of the ageing, the psychology of behaviour and computer science with clothing and textile design. A User Reference Group (URG) of male and female walkers within the 60–75-year-old age group was recruited within a 30-mile radius of the lead university. Co-design engagement embraced project partners, older research participants and a breadth of industry stakeholders from the outdoor clothing sector, including garment manufacturers, materials suppliers and technology developers. An iterative co-design process informed the practical design development of a garment 'layering system' from identification of user requirement, through design specification, garment engineering and the incorporation of technologies, to verification of the usability of the garment system and of the technology interface.

Co-design process

Following ethical procedures, strategies within the co-design process included: preparatory workshops for the development of a cross-disciplinary language; focus groups to explore the views of older research participants; and industrial liaison for access to specialist materials and processes for development of working prototypes. Initial 'show and tell' workshops uncovered users' perceptions in relation to available functional clothing, and textile and fibre innovation, as well as their understanding of wearable electronics. The concept of the sports-type layering system was introduced by researchers and industry stakeholders (Figure 3.2). A series of co-design workshops was held to identify in a systematic way the requirements of older users in relation to the layering system, in terms of style,

Figure 3.2: The sports layering system.
Image: David Taylor.

design detail and fabrication. Initial user bias towards natural fibres gave way to an interest in the lightweight comfort and easy-care attributes of modern fibres. Garment sizing was a particular user concern.

Capturing body shape and size

Understanding the size and shape of older consumers is not normally a concern of the mainstream fashion designer. This was the first study to use anthropometric data from the SizeUK survey (carried out between 2001 and 2004) to target the changing body shape of the 60–75-year-old age group. Information from the SizeUK database is not in the public domain but the project had an agreement with Sizemic Ltd to have access to details of the average body shapes and measurements that represented four of the five listed standard Body Mass Index (BMI) categories (underweight, normal, overweight, obese) to guide the selection of the research participants.

The process of capturing measurement by means of 3D body scanning was explained to the research participants. From an original group of 100, a sample for laser scanning was selected, using 32 men and women whose BMI closely resembled the averages identified in the database. The 3D scans of the sample were mapped to compare with those of the average 3D scans obtained from the database. Four men and four women, those with the most appropriate scan shapes, were invited to represent the target group (with a reserve for each BMI category). Basic 2D patterns were automatically generated from the chosen 3D scans to represent the true size and shape of the selected participants. These basic blocks were then adapted to address articulated cutting for movement for both functional and style requirements. Appropriate shape and fit would have obvious implications on the overall co-ordination and comfort of the garment layering system comprising base, mid and outer layers.

Style lines

The active ageing consider that current ranges look very similar, yet with size and fit that is unpredictable. The demand in the study was for fewer and less transitory styles to be available in more considered fit, in a wider size range, and with a greater choice of colours, fabrics and textures. Users were concerned with subtle, flattering style lines sympathetic to older figure types, as opposed to following dramatic swings in fashion. They expressed the need for more inclusive sizing, to extend from extra small to extra large sizes, and a choice of garment lengths to cater for variation in height and sleeve and leg length.

The principle of cutting in the round, to address the ergonomics of movement, was a particular consideration. Design lines were created to accommodate the demands of changing shape and posture, related garment balance and the limited flexibility of the older body. The putting on and taking off of garments required ease of movement, achieved through innovative cutting to provide articulation and arm lift, and further enhanced by introducing stretch and directional bias. Industry partners collaborated in the co-design selection of relatively lightweight and easy-care materials (Figure 3.3). Garment detailing, such as hood adjustment and pocket openings and closures, was cut with consideration of the reduced strength and dexterity of older wearers.

Fabric selection

The active ageing generation have seen the advent of modern fibres and fabrics during their lifetime. Some have a suspicion of synthetics due to the early poor

Figure 3.3: Co-design workshop with all stakeholders: industry, academia and users.
Photograph: David Taylor.

image of materials such as Bri-nylon, and presume that cotton and wool are 'natural' and 'good' while synthetic and man made fibres are 'bad'. Many have adopted functional textiles such as polyester fleeces and fabrics with waterproof or breathable finishes as the everyday dress of the population as a whole has become increasingly casual. However, many end-users lack an understanding of the benefit of moisture-wicking base layers. A major benefit of fibre development has been the introduction of elastane and mechanical stretch fibres that enhance fit, support, ease of movement, comfort and shape retention.

Involving older users in co-design stakeholder training for the shared understanding of materials, processes and terminologies across the disparate research disciplines resulted in greater confidence in the uptake of the comfort attributes of new materials. The 'body mapping' of fibre and fabric constructions, selected to maintain the homeostasis of the older body, provided enhanced breathability, thermal regulation and differing levels of protection, to contribute to overall comfort. Design decisions with regard to fabric selection were influenced by texture, handle and drape, seen to enhance the end-user 'feel-good factor'.

Colour

In garment selection, the active ageing participants were influenced by colour and texture in combination with age-appropriate size, fit and proportion (Figure 3.4). They welcomed less transient and extreme colour swings than those driven by relentless fashion trend. They were attracted to kinder and more enduring colours considered sympathetic to the ageing complexion and changing hair colour. They liked cheerful colours, avoiding the current predominance of black within the fashion trade. If they found an attractive and enduring style they admitted they would frequently buy two or more garments – in several colours, if appropriate.

Wearable technology

Co-design engagement introduced greater awareness of available technologies as well as the shortcomings in the functionality of garments not sufficiently user-ready to be reliable in the 'real world'. All participants were keen to experiment, despite the fact that user feedback displays were sometimes difficult to read and soft controls too closely positioned for those with reduced dexterity.

Figure 3.4: Colour design direction.
Photograph: David Taylor.

Design specification

The Design for Ageing Well practical research benefited from industrial liaison for the development of garment prototypes both in the UK and overseas. The detachment of clothing designers in the West from offshore production, with associated language barriers, demanded clear design specification to inform garment prototype development (Figure 3.5). The application of wearable electronics within the layering system was an additional challenge. The 'new' hybrid specification process required in merging electronics into garments demanded presentation skills including traditional drawing, computer aided illustration, 2D pattern cutting, 3D development on the mannequin, pattern digitisation and sample prototyping. This broad mix of skills enabled clear communication of the garment design detail to industry stakeholders to inform successful manufacture of the clothing layering system. The garment specification 'packages' were developed through knowledge transfer from the study backgrounds of a product designer and an architect, both new to clothing design.

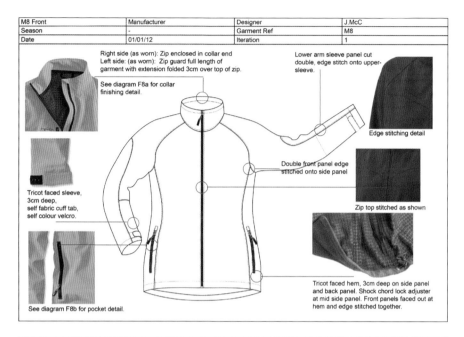

M8 Front	Manufacturer	Designer	J.McC
Season	-	Garment Ref	M8
Date	01/01/12	Iteration	1

Right side (as worn): Zip enclosed in collar end
Left side: (as worn): Zip guard full length of
garment with extension folded 3cm over top of zip.

See diagram F8a for collar
finishing detail.

Lower arm sleeve panel cut
double, edge stitch onto upper-
sleeve.

Edge stitching detail

Double front panel edge
stitched onto side panel

Tricot faced sleeve,
3cm deep,
self fabric cuff tab,
self colour velcro.

Zip top stitched as shown

Tricot faced hem, 3cm deep on side panel
and back panel. Shock chord lock adjuster
at mid side panel. Front panels faced out at
hem and edge stitched together.

See diagram F8b for pocket detail.

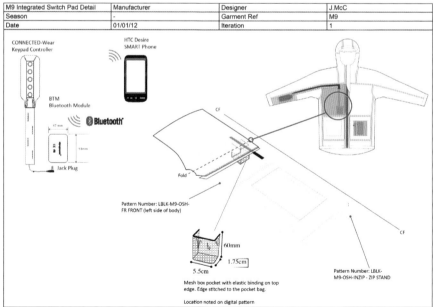

M9 Integrated Switch Pad Detail	Manufacturer	Designer	J.McC
Season	-	Garment Ref	M9
Date	01/01/12	Iteration	1

CONNECTED-Wear
Keypad Controller

HTC Desire
SMART Phone

BTM
Bluetooth Module

47 mm

Bluetooth

Jack Plug

CF

Fold

Pattern Number: LBLK-M9-OSH-
FR.FRONT (left side of body)

60mm

1.75cm

5.5cm

Mesh box pocket with elastic binding on top
edge. Edge stitched to the pocket bag.

Location noted on digital pattern

CF

Pattern Number: LBLK-
M9-OSH-INZIP - ZIP STAND

Figure 3.5: Garment specification, and integration of technology.
Image: Chris Lewis.

Co-design communication

Practical design-led research confirmed the importance of clear communication between all stakeholders at every stage in the iterative process in order to develop fit-for-purpose product. Co-design engagement effectively helped to break down initial barriers between the research disciplines and older users, in aiding the development of a shared language in terms of both specialist terminology and ways of working. The co-design process enabled users to express their needs and to learn of new product propositions and, in turn, has allowed researchers better to understand end-user needs, aspirations and limitations, as regards both clothing and technology devices.

Co-design research confirmed the importance of the designer's role in providing expert knowledge that other stakeholders do not have. It has shown that technical clothing design can benefit from the input of design practitioners from disciplines other than fashion design. Product, architecture, graphic and web designers, as researchers, contributed to empowering lay participants in the visual expression of their creativity and in supporting contributions to practical creative development. Designers with practical technical skills were needed to incorporate new and emerging technologies, and provide an overview of production processes and business contexts as relevant, throughout the iterative design process. Co-design 'offers an opportunity for multi-stakeholders to collectively define the context and problem and in doing so improve the chances of a design outcome being effective'. A team approach may embrace varying combinations of elements contributing to underlying design philosophy, processes, methodologies and tools (Fuad-Luke 2009).

Conclusion: the way forward

It was encouraging to find the lead article in the launch issue of the sports trade magazine *ISPO News* (Grober 2012) discussing the health and fitness of the ageing consumer. The front cover depicted an upbeat image of active agers with the caption 'Live Healthy, Live Longer'. Editor Tobias Grober quoted Professor Christoph Bamberger's suggestion that 'People who are physically active throughout their lives remain younger and healthier longer'. Bamberger believes that 'our genes are not the only factor determining whether we live happily to an advanced age. Prevention and lifestyle are much more important.' Since then the leading outdoor trade event has held seminars with speakers including Dr William Bird, of Intelligent Health,[3] to promote wellbeing associated with exercise in the countryside, and the UK Outdoor Industry Association has launched its 'Britain on Foot'[4] campaign (October 2012). Significantly, the 'Design for Ageing Well' project was invited to have a stand within the 'ISPO HealthStyle' exhibition.

In terms of marketing, 'Some great brands have come about by companies treating their customers as people not as data sets' (Wolfe and Snyder 2003). However, the undeniable fact is that many brands still focus on young people. Older people do not respond to marketing hype. A better approach, says Chris Arnold, is:

> people want to be engaged. By working together with the consumer you show genuine commitment as well as developing a relationship. The consumer really does want to be part of the solution and if you facilitate that they'll love you for it. It's all about shared responsibility.

> (2009: 84)

WPP executive Sir Martin Sorrell told *Marketing Week* that 'Baby boomers are where the wealth and income is. I don't know whether you can aim at both boomers and younger groups or whether you have to use more segmented and targeted strategies. But you ignore either at your peril' (Handley 2011). The dangerous assumption of a lot of advertisers is: 'We'll advertise younger and these people will come along for the ride' (ibid.). Beth Brady, global head of Nielsen Marketing (a company which conducted research on 'boomers') says, 'This group is redefining aging. … They grew up in the age of consumerism. Their sheer size helped define brands; they're rebellious'. The report points out, 'this is not your grandma' (Huffington Post 2012).

In relation to the image of ageing, a German government report states that 'It is worth taking a new look at old age' in acknowledging that older people are under-represented in television films and advertising. 'In public debate, demographic change is often associated with negative attributes and depicted as a threat'. However 'A portrayal by the media showing old age in all its diversity and relationships between the generations in all their diverse aspects, on the other hand, contributes greatly to a responsible attitude towards the challenges of demographic change' (German Federal Ministry for Family Affairs 2011). The term 'old age' should be replaced by 'ageing' with the life course perspective more clearly emphasised. 'In developing and designing products and their advertising and marketing, the consumer industry should give great attention to the development of individual needs over the entire life course' (ibid.).

Ellen Peters suggests that 'Because older adults are, by virtue of age, closer to the end of life, age should be associated with an increased importance of emotional goals; increased attention to emotional content; and either an increased focus on positive information or a decreased focus on negative information to optimize emotional experience' (Peters 2010). In Design for Ageing Well many older research participants referred to a garment that they had grown to love, often with meaningful associations, as 'an old friend'. This was often to do with personal style as opposed to fashion. In 'Clothes: A Manifesto', Willis reports that in her survey, '"Style" trumped fashion overwhelmingly. … That's because style is personal, and − crucially − something that can't be bought. No one admits to striving to look "fashionable"; they would prefer to look "well-dressed", "considered", "confident", but above all "stylish"'(Willis 2013).

This chapter has discussed strategies for involving the active ageing, as the new consumer majority, in a new co-design approach to addressing their technical, aesthetic and socio-cultural clothing design needs and aspirations. The author identifies whole-heartedly with the following views on the importance of design:

> The real JOY of design is to deliver fresh perspectives, improved wellbeing and an intuitive sense of balance with the wider world. The real RELEVANCE of design is its ability to be proactive. The real PASSION of design is in its philosophical, ethical and practical debate.
>
> (Fuad-Luke 2009)

Notes

1 www.size.org (accessed 4 July 2014).
2 www.newdynamics.group.shef.ac.uk/design-for-ageing.html (accessed 4 July 2014).
3 www.intelligenthealth.co.uk (accessed 4 July 2014).
4 www.britainonfoot.co.uk (accessed 4 July 2014).

References

Arnold, C. (2009) *Ethical Marketing and the New Consumer*, Chichester, UK: John Wiley and Sons.

Cambridge Engineering Design Centre (EDC) (2005) Identifying User Wants, Cambridge: CUED Multimedia Group. Available online at: www.eng.cam.ac.uk/inclusivedesign/index.php?section=design (accessed 3 March 2014).

Coates, J. (2005) From My Perspective: The Future of Clothing, *Technological Forecasting & Social Change*, 72 (1): 101–110.

Design Council (n.d.) Inclusive Design Education Resource, London: Design Council. Available online at: www.designcouncil.info/inclusivedesign resource/ (accessed 3 March 2014).

The Economist (2002) Marketing to the Old: Over 60 and Overlooked. Available online at: www.economist.com/node/1270771 (accessed 3 March 2014).

Fuad-Luke, A. (2009) *Design Activism: Beautiful Strangeness for a Sustainable World*, London: Sterling, VA: Earthscan.

German Federal Ministry for Family Affairs, Senior Citizens, Women and Youth (BMFSFJ) (2011) *A New Culture of Ageing: Images of Ageing in Society. Findings and Recommendations of the Sixth German Government Report on the Elderly*. Bonn: BMFSFJ. Available online at: www.dza.de/en/policy-consulting/office-of-the-government-reports/previous-reports-on-older-people.html (accessed 4 July 2014).

Grober, T. (2012) Live Healthy, Live Longer. Interview with Christoph M. Bamberger, *ISPO News* magazine, 2 (January).

Handley, Lucy (2011) Baby Boomers Key to Brand Segmentation, In-Depth Analysis, *Marketing Week*, 1 December. Available online at: www.marketingweek.co.uk/baby-boomers-key-to-brand-segmentation/3032343.article (accessed 21 April 2013).

Huffington Post (2012) Boomers Are 'the Most Valuable Generation' for Marketers, Nielsen Report Finds. *Huffington Post*. Available online at: www.huffingtonpost.com/2012/08/17/marketing-to-boomers–most-valuable-generation_n_1791361.html (accessed 3 March 2014).

McCann, J. (1999) *Establishing the Requirements for the Design Development of Performance Sportswear*. M.Phil. thesis (unpublished). Derby, UK: University of Derby.

McCann, J. (2009) End-User Based Design of Innovative Smart Clothing. In: McCann, J. and Bryson, D. (eds) *Smart Clothes and Wearable Technology*. Cambridge, UK: Woodhead Publishing.

McCann, J. (2012) Translating the Hybrid Methodologies and Practical Outputs of Smart Textile-Oriented Research, in Clothing for the Growing Ageing Market, for the Benefit of All Stakeholders. In *Proceedings of the 88th Textile Institute World Conference, Bridging Innovation, Research and Enterprise*, 15–17 May, Shah Alam, Selangor, Malaysia.

McCann, J. (2013) UK Manufacturing Potential for the New Consumer Majority, the Active Ageing? *ASBCI Magazine*.

Metz, D. and Underwood, M. (2005) *Older Richer Fitter: Identifying the Customer Needs of Britain's Ageing Population*. London: Age Concern Books.

Moody, H. R. and Sood, S. (2010) Age Branding. In Drolet, A., Schwarz, N. and Yoon, C. (eds) *The Ageing Consumer: Perspectives from Psychology and Economics*. New York: Routledge.

Peters, E. (2010) Ageing-Related Changes in Decision Making. In Drolet, A., Schwarz, N. and Yoon, C. (eds) *The Ageing Consumer: Perspectives from Psychology and Economics*. New York: Routledge.

Rutherford, T. (2012) Population Ageing: Statistics, SN/SG/3228, House of Commons Library Standard Note, Social and General Statistics. Available online at: www.parliament.uk/briefing-papers/sn03228.pdf (accessed 4 July 2014).

Sanders, E. and Stappers, P. (2008) Co-Creation and the New Landscapes of Design, *CoDesign*, 4 (1): 5–18.

Thomas, L. (2012) Nation of Bad Dressers: Everyone Looks the Same and Their Clothes Have Never Been So Ugly, Says Vivienne Westwood. *Daily Mail*, 20 February. Available online at: www.dailymail.co.uk/femail/article-2103601/Vivienne-Westwood-Everyone-looks-clothes-ugly.html#ixzz1pNp2lIkZ (accessed 24 September 2012).

Whitehorn, K. (2012) Vivienne Westwood May Think Women Are Stylish at 70 – but Where's the Help? *The Guardian*, 20 February. Available online at: www.guardian.co.uk/commentisfree/2012/feb/20/vivienne-westwood-stylish-70 (accessed 4 July 2014).

Willis, R. (2013) Clothes: A Manifesto. *Intelligent Life* magazine, March/April. Available online at: http://moreintelligentlife.com/content/lifestyle/rebecca-willis/clothes-a-manifesto?page=full (accessed 3 March 2014).

Wolfe, D. B. and Snyder, R. E. (2003) *Ageless Marketing: Strategies for Reaching the Hearts and Minds of the New Customer Majority*. Chicago: Dearborn.

Chapter Four

Fashion and sustainability
Repairing the clothes we wear

Alison Gwilt, Sheffield Hallam University, UK

Introduction

This chapter discusses and explores the role that design-led approaches can perform in encouraging people to (re-)engage with clothing repair. Each year approximately 350,000 tonnes of used clothing is sent to UK landfills but research suggests that this figure could be significantly reduced if wearers were actively and routinely to repair damaged clothes (WRAP 2012). As leaders within the fashion industry strive to improve the production of fashion clothing through cleaner/more efficient/more ethical processes, this chapter looks at the part that designers and consumers can play in utilizing garment life cycle extension strategies, as a way of reducing unnecessary textile waste.

Before the Second World War, in Europe and America, clothing was routinely repaired and altered, either in the home or through a service provider. Garments were considered valuable items and, mainly for economic reasons, they were regularly repaired. Labour costs associated with repairing were at the time affordable in comparison to the price of new materials and garments (Gwilt and Rissanen 2011). As the ready-to-wear market flourished in the 1960s, fashion became increasingly affordable and accessible, which facilitated a decline in the traditional culture of mending and altering clothes. Repairing clothes began to be considered as time consuming and expensive in comparison to the availability and price of new clothes. This view quickly became the social norm in developed western cultures and still remains largely accepted amongst contemporary society, which on the whole no longer engages with clothing repair as a matter of routine (Fisher *et al.* 2008).

61

However, some contemporary approaches to fashion design are beginning to provide designers with the opportunity to reinvigorate domestic mending practices, whilst exploring new models of business practice. But it is through an understanding of the attitudes and practices of wearers towards clothing repair that designers will gain the insight to influence change in use practices. This chapter discusses some of the design–led approaches that designers can employ to encourage clothing repair, and profiles the 'Make Do and Mend' clothing repair study conducted by an interdisciplinary team of researchers at Sheffield Hallam University.

Fashion for sustainability

Fashion designing for sustainability involves engaging in strategies and approaches that can help reduce or avoid the social, environmental, economic and cultural impacts associated with the production and consumption of fashion clothing. The fashion industry, as it stands, contributes to the use of natural resources, such as fossil fuels, to create energy for production processes which release toxic emissions into the atmosphere. At the same time, water is depleted for crop cultivation, textile processing and laundering, and some of these processes pollute our waterways with chemicals (Allwood *et al.* 2006). In the garment factories, where employment should be considered positive, the pay and working conditions for many people are poor. These, along with other negative impacts, are consequences of the activities involved in the five distinct phases in the life cycle of a garment: design; production; distribution; use; and end-of-life.

During the design phase the fashion designer, in some shape or form, can – directly or indirectly – influence changes across many other phases of a garment's life cycle, and so can play a positive part in improving the fashion process. In the fashion industry there have been a number of designers, such as Stella McCartney, Safia Minney (People Tree) and Vivienne Westwood, who, along with manufacturers and retailers like Marks and Spencer, Patagonia, Nike and H&M, have embarked on sustainability programmes in an effort to improve the environmental and ethical performance of their products and services. Although it is important for all sectors of the fashion industry to create sustainable products and services, it is society's fascination for consuming fashion goods that is of greatest concern. In comparison with garment production and consumption patterns in previous decades, fashion is now more accessible and affordable (Welters 2008). This is in part due to the increased availability of low quality, inexpensive products, which provide the cost-conscious consumer with an affordable 'fashion fix' (ibid.). However, these products are typically constructed from inferior fabrics and materials, and manufactured in factories where employees have poor working conditions and low salaries. At the same time, the established fashion industry cycle means that new fashion products (inexpensive or not) are developed for the new seasonal collections, which are deliberately designed with a 'built-in obsolescence', fuelling the consumer's need for regular consumption. Although this over production of fashion garments needs to be questioned, the accompanying view that fashion is 'disposable' is also of great concern. All too often designers intentionally develop garments that persuade the consumer to discard one garment in pursuit of another. While the continual development of new garments may make economic sense to fashion producers, it is ultimately destructive to society and the environment. The question is, how do we begin to change these accepted attitudes, and how can we reduce or avoid the textile waste going to landfill while we continue to produce and sell new products?

Positive improvements in production

In some areas of the fashion industry, over the last decade, there has been a significant move to tackle the impacts of manufacturing. Industry leaders, non-governmental organizations (NGOs), campaigners and advocates are raising awareness, promoting engagement and profiling improvements that can assist design teams to use (for example) efficient processes, and responsible sourcing and manufacturing. Many designers now have a greater acceptance of, and access to, sustainable fibres and fabrics as they make key selections during the design phase. Specialist agencies are sourcing fabrics and materials from textile mills and manufacturers that use low impact processes or work with fair trade farmers and growers. During the garment production phase, fashion companies are now partnering with ethical manufacturers, and in the manufacturing facility recycling of textile waste has, for several producers, become a matter of routine, with some of the pre-consumer waste becoming the primary material resource for an increasing number of fashion labels (Black 2012). Although several innovative waste reduction approaches, such as zero waste patternmaking, are in their infancy within the industry, it is argued that the real achievement lies with the recent increased awareness of sustainability issues across the sector (ibid.). Within the fashion community many are now aware of the general issues related to the impacts of production, and there is a greater understanding that improvements, however small, are needed in this area. Frequently the fashion designer is seen as a key contributor in this respect. However, while much visibility is given to making improvements across the design and production stages, there is a general lack of awareness of design-led approaches that can be used to influence improvements after the point of sale and during use. A significant amount of textile waste is generated during use, because wearers discard clothing for a number of different reasons; however, much of this waste could be reduced if attitudes and practices regarding clothing care were to improve (WRAP 2012).

Improving practices during use

How do we use clothes?

Bras-Klapwijk and Knot (2001) suggest that the 'use' phase of a garment can be separated into a series of activities: wearing, washing, storing, repairing (adaption and alteration) and disposal. A number of studies have noted that it is during the use phase in the life cycle of a fashion garment that most of the environmental impacts occur (Fletcher 2008; Black 2012). However, each person develops a clothing care and maintenance routine based on personal patterns of use, which may be different to the practice employed by others. This means that the way that garments are cared for can be vastly different between one user and the next; for example, clothes may be laundered carefully or badly, or they may be discarded too readily before repair or alteration possibilities are considered.

Why do patterns of use matter?

There is a direct relationship between the practices applied during use and the creation of textile waste. Although the spread of inexpensive products is highlighted as a contributing factor in the rising amounts of textile waste, it is apparent that garments, irrespective of price or quality, are discarded for a variety of reasons. For example, wearers might discard a garment because of product boredom as much as issues related to damage or problems with fit. The destination of a discarded garment depends on the philosophical viewpoint of the wearer, but in a survey conducted by WRAP (2012) more than half the adults interviewed admitted that garments were placed in the bin, typically because they were perceived to have no value.

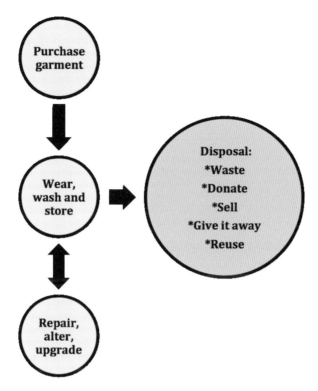

Figure 4.1: Diagram based on the clothing care function.
Source: Adapted from Bras-Klapwijk and Knot 2001.

According to Allwood *et al.* (2006), almost 74 per cent of the textile waste that is created is sent to landfill. Included in this definition of textile waste are items of fashion clothing, many of which could be reused or recycled, with obvious benefits to the environment and a reduction in the cost of resources needed to manufacture new products (WRAP 2012). Moreover, the WRAP report suggests that if the active use of a garment increased to approximately three years (in the UK it is currently 2.2 years), there would be a saving of between 20 and 30 per cent each for carbon, water and waste footprints. These statistics reveal that while a high level of material waste, produced as a consequence of use, is going to landfill, there are benefits to be had in employing garment extension strategies. This is where the fashion designer can make a significant contribution, since it is argued that during the design process it is possible to consider the relationship between the designed garment and its journey after the point of sale.

Existing examples of design-led approaches to repair

During the design process designers can embed approaches that support or improve the wearer's attitudes and practices towards clothing repair during use. At the outset of the design process the designer can profile a specific approach to the use of a garment that can be achieved through either an industry or a domestic lens; for example, the wearer can be empowered to carry out a repair personally or be steered towards a specialist repair service. Although the opportunity to engage with clothing repair has always existed, it is through the uptake of innovative design-led approaches that we may be able to change established cultural attitudes to repair and encourage wearers to (re-)engage with mending practices. Although this may appear to be a twenty-first-century problem and concept, there are many existing examples of innovative approaches to mending to be found in historical dress and costume collections.

When we examine period garments it is apparent that, typically, repair work was only undertaken when it was necessary; however, a wide range of clothes was designed from the outset to accommodate later alterations and/or repairs. For example, in some varieties of seventeenth-century dress, garment sleeves or cuffs were created as detachable pieces so that the items could be efficiently washed, repaired and/or replaced with ease (Hart and North 1998). Historical garments also reveal the need for repairs to mask damage. Mending practices traditionally focused on hiding damage, particularly if the garment was considered precious or valuable. The extent of the techniques used to accomplish repair work was varied and dependent on the wearer's access to skills and materials, and on the social and cultural norms of the time.

However, throughout the history of domestic mending individual wearers have frequently adopted a creative approach to repairing, and have developed strategies that embrace a variety of skills, materials and resources. This is particularly demonstrated in the Second World War government-led 'Make Do and Mend' campaigns in the US and UK. Techniques such as darning, patching and repurposing were promoted as creative and resourceful strategies for reusing fabrics and garments. Educational campaign leaflets were developed to provide the public with useful advice on the best approaches to clothing care and repair, and promoted inventive thinking in this respect since materials and new garments were in short supply. From many of the UK Board of Trade pamphlets it was apparent that the use of invisible mending techniques required a good level of skill, so further support was provided through a council-run evening class service (UK Ministry of Information 1943). Throughout the Second World War and early post-war period mending clothing was considered a responsible action that benefited the nation.

However, the invisible repair of clothing has not always been perceived as necessary. This attitude is evident in clothing worn by specific sub-culture groups, such as the Punks of the 1970s, where resistance created extreme results. This anarchic movement challenged conventional styles of dress by adopting aggressively styled clothing that proudly embraced and purposely inserted rips, tears and stains. UK designer Vivienne Westwood, particularly associated with early Punk clothing, exploited these concepts in garments designed to shock (Laver 2002). This anti-fashion concept continued to appear in fashion; in the late 1980s Japanese designer Rei Kawakubo, with her label Comme des Garçons, incorporated randomly placed holes in monochromatic knitwear pieces, while in the 1990s Belgian designer Martin Margiela used exposed seams and slash details to create deconstructed pieces that signalled a distressed style.

In postdigital contemporary fashion, within online and offline communities, there has been a resurgence of craft practices that has led to a renewed interest in creative alteration of clothing. Although this is happening at a time when the notion of mending seems to have all but disappeared from the cultural landscape, some sectors of society have begun to acknowledge the environmental and social benefits of repairing clothes. Unfortunately this view tends to sit outside mainstream thinking; the dominant belief is that damaged clothing should be discarded rather than repaired. Consequently there is still much work to be done if we are to motivate and encourage a wider range of people to (re-)engage with mending practices.

A study of attitudes and practices concerning clothing repair

In 2013 an interdisciplinary team of researchers at Sheffield Hallam University conducted a clothing repair study, Make, Do and Mend.[1] The aim of the pilot study was to understand what people think and know about clothing repair, and to bring to the foreground mechanisms to support and encourage engagement in mending practices. Our objective was two-fold: first, to look for approaches that may reinvigorate community-based clothing repair activity; and second, to identify the roles that online and offline activities play in facilitating knowledge exchange. The pilot study was driven by three main research questions, which focused on

Figure 4.2: Mending the hole in a t-shirt.
The 'Make, Do and Mend' study, Sheffield Hallam University; photography Outradius Media.

understanding a) what people think and know about clothing repair; b) what people currently do with damaged clothes; and c) what is needed to support and encourage people to engage in repairing. At the outset of the study it was essential that we understood the attitudes of wearers to clothing repair and the practices that people currently use. Apart from the instructional texts and resources that provide technical information about mending, there has been little research conducted to compare the attitudes of wearers with actual ability or behaviour. In order to identify the mechanisms that would support engagement, it was necessary to reveal and compare these two positions. Although the intention of the study was to focus on encouraging mending within the domestic environment, an underlying aim was to see the potential for mending within an industry perspective, particularly in identifying opportunities for designers.

Initially we conducted surveys distributed amongst online sewing/craft forums, groups and networks and the local community in an attempt to capture a general picture of attitudes towards the repair of clothing. We asked people what they currently do with damaged clothes; what their motivations were for repairing; what barriers they faced; and what support was needed. We also sought to uncover whether gender, cultural or generational differences would impact on the wearer's opinions and behaviour. At the same time we observed the physical approaches of wearers to mending a garment in two practical workshops. Designed to accommodate different levels of technical ability, the workshops required participant volunteer menders to self-elect and enrol in either the novice mender session or the amateur mender workshop session. For the purposes of this study we described the novice mender as a person with little or no sewing experience, while the amateur was considered a proficient sewer or repairer. The task for the menders involved repairing a hole in either a pair of denim jeans or a cotton t-shirt to what they considered a wearable standard. The research team selected these particular items of clothing – jeans and a t-shirt – on the premise that they are two basic items found in most wardrobes. The menders were provided with a range of basic and specialist sewing equipment (needles, thread, fabric, fusible web, decorative trims), household and stationery items (sticky tape, staples, glue) and resources such as a sewing machine, a computer and books. During the workshop sessions we conducted interviews with the menders, while they had to capture their thoughts, decisions (and lack of decision), dilemmas and trials through a visual documentation task (see Figure 4.3).

Although our intention was to observe the menders' approach and ability (creative and technical), we also wanted to understand the relevance and significance of the tools and resources used to complete the task. For example, what impact did creativity or skill have on the final outcome? And did the resources support the approach taken? Moreover, we wanted to identify differences between

Figure 4.3: Planning and documenting the repair task.
The 'Make, Do and Mend' study, Sheffield Hallam University; photography Outradius Media.

the novice and the amateur menders; and would the approaches of individual and grouped participants differ? How did the participants feel about the task? Throughout the task it became clear that there is a need to consider the appearance of a repaired garment; this prompted thoughts such as, how do we measure good repair skills, and by whose standards? As the study progressed it was clear that this was a significant point of concern, which was also in evidence in the workshop self-enrolment exercise (based on self-assessed levels of skill), where typically the menders' views of their own abilities or knowledge were different from that of the researchers.

What we discovered

In dress and costume history, wearing repaired clothing was typically a signifier of financial hardship, particularly when the repair was visible. This notion has continued to influence contemporary thinking about repair and it is one of the challenges that we need to overcome if we are to make the wearing of repaired clothing more socially acceptable. Encouraging people to wear garments that have been repaired, particularly if the repair is visible, is for many people unacceptable (Fletcher 2008). In the workshop sessions we wondered whether the volunteer menders would conceal the damage in a garment or allow it to remain visible as a demonstration of individuality. Would the menders enhance and enrich stains, holes and tears, using decorative techniques, or would they opt for invisible repair methods? Our observations in the practical workshop sessions appeared very different from the data collected in our survey. Amongst our survey respondents almost 82 per cent had a preference for invisible garment repairs; however, while the volunteer menders verbally echoed this point in the workshop sessions, in their own practical application most had used visible mending techniques. Although some of our menders proposed to hide damage behind a cloth patch, the patch itself was clearly visible, almost decorative. On further analysis it would seem that these contradictions might in part be due to a lack (or perceived lack) of skill, which in our survey and interview data was identified as a major barrier to engaging with repair work. Despite a general enthusiasm for repairing damaged clothing, there is an established cultural belief system that promotes the need for invisibility in clothing repair, which usually requires a high level of technical skill. Although the technical skills required for invisible mending may be seen as a barrier to engagement in repair practices for the majority of people, the opportunity for

Figure 4.4: Applying a clothing patch to hide garment damage.
The 'Make, Do and Mend' study, Sheffield Hallam University; photography Outradius Media.

creative approaches offered by visible mending could help wearers (re)connect with mending. However, while the issue of lack of skill is important, it is the perceived difficulty or stigma associated with wearing 'visibly' repaired clothing that is a matter for concern.

As we explored the mechanisms needed to support people in clothing repair, we established from our data that wearers consider a combination of online and offline 'resources' as valuable. For example, despite the availability of specific resources (such as texts, workshops, short courses or formal online groups), many wearers will initially seek advice from a family member and/or the Internet. At the same time, our volunteer menders highlighted the benefits to personal wellbeing when attending the workshop. Despite no practical guidance or support from the researchers, the menders felt that the workshop experience was pleasurable and provided the time and access to resources to conduct repair work that gave them a sense of personal achievement. This point was in stark contrast to perceptions of solitary domestic repairing; the survey data revealed that repairing clothes at home was at times considered to be a time consuming 'chore'.

Throughout the pilot study we began to identify issues and barriers that affect a wearer's relationship with clothing repair, while at the same time starting to identify some of the mechanisms that may provide support. The study also revealed the difficulty in attracting data representative of a wider variety of people. Although 200 respondents engaged with our online survey, the number of respondents under the age of 25 or representing the male population was smaller than anticipated. However, we found that the number of male and younger respondents increased dramatically when we conducted interviews and surveys at a small public exhibition of the research findings. It is apparent that getting out and amongst the community is critical in order to capture an extensive and accurate picture of attitudes and practices.

From data to design

Stressing the importance of understanding the attitudes and practices surrounding use can help shape and inform the development of new modes of practice, for example 'product-service system' models. Predictions for the fashion industry often highlight the role that product and service combinations will play in establishing resource efficient consumption modes (Bras-Klapwijk and Knot 2001; WRAP 2012). For fashion designers this could lead to a new model of design practice embracing service approaches that might involve leasing, repairing, remodelling or re-manufacturing activities which sit alongside or in place of traditional production and distribution paradigms. In the examples of design-led approaches found in historical dress, discussed earlier, it is evident that there are existing methods from dress and costume history which may support contemporary society in reconnecting with repair practices. For example, the notion of modularity provides contemporary designers with an efficient approach to the use of materials and resources, while for the wearer it improves the accessibility to the damaged area, and provides a greater opportunity for creative intervention without the need to discard or disrupt the entire garment. The garment's adaptability provides the wearer with a product that is 'value-added' and which is regarded as competitive in price. The potential to develop garments that actively facilitate the repairing, altering or replacing of components offers obvious benefits to the wearer and the environment. However, what is noteworthy is the designer's ability, through the creative application of these concepts, to influence positively society's attitudes towards wearing repaired garments. There are many different ways in which the designer can creatively 'promote' visibly repaired clothing, but perhaps repairing does not have to take place at all. It may be timely to suggest that there is a need to accept as a society that clothing will age and that this in itself may (positively) signify a valued empathetic relationship between wearer and garment. Garment designs that make use of deflective devices such as intentional stains, rips, tears and holes provide the fashion designer with the opportunity to develop clothes that embrace future damage, leaving it untouched and unnoticed. This allows us to question whether garments can accrue value through their associations with the wearer, and whether wear and tear may be evidence of this value. To some extent this has been previously witnessed in fashion: in the 1980s there was a phenomenon of damaged, vintage Levi's 501 jeans, which retailed at a far higher price than the newly manufactured product (Wilson and Taylor 1989). These possibilities, amongst others, provide new potential dimensions to the business practices of a fashion company.

Figure 4.5: Textural patterns hide damage in Bruno Kleist's menswear. Danish designer Kleist developed a natural dye process from materials such as fungus, compost and iron.
Photographer: Michael Kim Nguyen.

73

The measure of success for many fashion producers is grounded in the economics generated by the production and consumption of fashion goods. The fashion system is still predominantly made up of a (global) network of producers, manufacturers, designers and retailers, but rather than see this simply as an industry related to production it is timely to consider the notion of a community connected to use. A community connected to use will support a growth in fashion product-service business models. The fashion product-service model can play an important role in transforming our attitudes and behaviours towards clothing, and may improve the disconnection between designer and wearer apparent in large-scale manufacturing. By bridging the gap between designer and wearer it may be possible to reduce the (wasteful) over production of garments and encourage the wearer to become an active participant in the world of fashion garments in a way that extends the role of the owner beyond the basic position of consumer. For the

Figure 4.6: London-based designers Queenie and Ted upcycle damaged garments to specific customer requirements.
Photographer: Nicola Tree.

designer it becomes important to reject the conventional approach to the creative process, which involves designing from an external (professional) perspective, and move to designing from an internal (user) perspective (Gwilt 2013). By adopting this perspective we are better positioned to explore and challenge the way that garments are created, used and discarded. The fashion community concept may also support the improved integration and interconnection of isolated members of the fashion community such as skilled artisans, non-profit enterprises, service providers, co-operatives, suppliers and user-led ventures, which may help move us away from the traditional fashion production–consumption system. This is a robust approach to rethinking the fashion industry status quo that may enable the fashion community to become an important part of local cultural life, where fashion is seen as something other than a homogenized product from large-scale manufacturing.

Conclusion

Reducing the environmental impacts associated with clothing use is best approached once the functions and tasks within the use phase of a garment are understood. Rather than rely on feedback from the sales team or retailer, designers would benefit from the insight gained directly from wearers. It is through this engagement that designers find new opportunities for innovation, and at the same time they are positioned to refine and redevelop products in response to the genuine needs of wearers. At a practice level the designer can begin by reflecting on their personal experience as a wearer, but the most powerful insight is best gained directly from wearers who have experienced and interacted with developed products.

Understanding the attitudes and behaviours of wearers during use provides designers with insight that may inform new products and/or business models which can support improvements in care routines. But it is also apparent that the transfer of knowledge between and amongst individuals and communities of wearers is of social benefit, and this is especially important given the need to reinvigorate an engagement with domestic mending practices. However, to encourage the sharing of mending knowledge amongst communities, those within the mainstream markets must first embrace the idea that wearing visibly and invisibly repaired garments is culturally acceptable. This process of normalization is a challenge that designers can tackle specifically through the use of innovative design-led approaches to new garment designs.

These points also bring to light the issue of personal responsibility; while the suggestion is that the designer can promote and support new attitudes towards clothing repair, there is a need for the wearer to engage in repair activities and to wear the repaired item. This is where it becomes important to think of fashion existing within a community rather than an industry; where we – suppliers, designers, producers, retailers, wearers, menders and recyclers – all have a part to play.

Note

1 The 'Make, Do and Mend' interdisciplinary study was funded by the 'Imagine' scheme at Sheffield Hallam University. For further project information visit www.shu.ac.uk/research/c3ri/projects/make-do-and-mend (accessed 18 March 2014).

References

Allwood, J. M., Laursen, S. E., Malvido de Rodríguez, C. and Bocken, N. M. P. (2006) *Well Dressed? The Present and Future Sustainability of Clothing and Textiles in the United Kingdom*, Cambridge: Institute for Manufacturing, University of Cambridge.

Black, S. (2012) *The Sustainable Fashion Handbook,* London: Thames & Hudson.

Bras-Klapwijk, R. M. and Knot, J. M. C. (2001) 'Strategic Environmental Assessment for Sustainable Households in 2050: Illustrated for Clothing', *Sustainable Development*, **9**(2), pp. 109–118.

Fisher, T., Cooper, T., Woodward, S., Hiller, A. and Goworek, H. (2008) *Public Understanding of Sustainable Clothing: A Report to the Department for Environment, Food and Rural Affairs*, London: DEFRA.

Fletcher, K. (2008) *Sustainable Fashion and Textiles: Design Journeys*, London: Earthscan.

Gwilt, A. (2013) 'Valuing The Role of the Wearer in the Creation of Sustainable Fashion', *Research Journal of Textile and Apparel*, **17**(1), pp. 78–86.

Gwilt, A. and Rissanen, T. (eds) (2011) *Shaping Sustainable Fashion: Changing the Way We Make and Use Clothes*, London: Earthscan.

Hart, A. and North, S. (1998) *Historical Fashion in Detail: the Seventeenth and Eighteenth Centuries*, London: V&A Publishing.

Laver, J. (2002) *Costume and Fashion: A Concise History*, London: Thames & Hudson. United Kingdom.

Ministry of Information (1943) *Make Do and Mend*, London: UK Board of Trade.

Welters, L. (2008) The Fashion of Sustainability. In: Hethorn, J. and Ulasewicz, C. (eds) *Sustainable Fashion: Why Now? A Conversation About Issues, Practices, and Possibilities*, New York: Fairchild Books.

Wilson, E. and Taylor, L. (1989) *Through the Looking Glass: A History of Dress from 1860 to the Present Day*, London: BBC Books.

WRAP (2012) 'Valuing Our Clothes: The True Cost of How We Design, Use and Dispose of Clothing in the UK', Banbury, UK: WRAP. Available online at: www.wrap.org.uk/sites/files/wrap/VoC%20FINAL%20online%202012%2007%2011.pdf (accessed 18 March 2014).

Chapter Five

Fashion design and fashion cooperatives
A case study of the Lydia Lavín brand

Lydia Lavín, Universidad Iberoamericana and Lydia Lavín brand, Mexico
Montserrat Messeguer Lavín, Lydia Lavín brand, Mexico

Mexico is renowned for some of the best examples of textile work that is produced by indigenous and mestizo communities. The groups often produce textiles that preserve traditions dating from the Pre-Columbian era and in many cases they still use traditional textiles for celebrations and in everyday life. Many of these communities have managed to maintain their lifestyles, language and traditions because of their geographic isolation.

Mexico was conquered in the sixteenth century by Spain; thereafter, the country went through a period of syncretism that resulted in important cultural, legal and religious changes that affected the way of being, thinking, looking, dressing and how we live generally. The indigenous communities that remained isolated were the ones who preserved their own traditions, since the Conquest took hundreds of years to reach them. The gradual arrival of roads, television and now the Internet to these remote regions has increasingly forced textile traditions to be abandoned or transformed. It has also made the arrival of new influences possible: techniques and materials that have initiated new mestizo traditions.

Today, there are active indigenous groups in many states of Mexico and most of them continue with pre-Hispanic practices, speak their own language and live their traditions.[1] Many of them have already been integrated into the culture created during the Conquest, which results in what we are as Mexicans now: a nation composed of a mostly mestizo population that speaks Spanish and is immersed in modernity. The states that currently have the largest indigenous populations are: Chiapas, Guerrero, Oaxaca, Puebla, the state of Mexico and Michoacán. The diversity of its geography and the fact that they belonged to pre-

Hispanic kingdoms with different origins from the Aztecs – the *Totonacos*, *Mixtecos*, *Zapotecos* and Mayans,[2] among others – results in ethnic cultures of great cultural richness and variety.

As two Mexican women, we feel very proud of having and being part of this great cultural mosaic that is Mexico. We are a Mexican mother and daughter and carry a mixture of Spanish, French, *Chichimeca*, *Tzotzil* and *Nahua* blood.[3]

Establishing the Lydia Lavín label

I, Lydia, studied two university degrees, one in Graphic Design and another in Textile Design. I had the opportunity to work, when I was young, with a well-known anthropologist and researcher of indigenous clothing, named Martha Turok. She invited me first as her student and then as a designer to conduct fieldwork in remote areas of Mexico. The work consisted of researching the textile traditions of various indigenous communities in the country and recording the information to avoid its loss. Eventually, I began teaching Traditional Mexican Textile Design at the Universidad Iberoamericana, a class of which I was head professor for 16 years. Later, I conducted work on the recovery of clothing and indigenous techniques that were disappearing; this work was carried out throughout ten years with the Indigenous Institute[4] and the FONART.[5]

I, Montserrat, Lydia's daughter, studied Textile Design and had the opportunity of doing a social service program in the state of Chiapas, working with *Chamula* and Tzotzil communities, especially on the subject of innovation. The plan was to support the commercial outlet of products with design. Two years ago, after having finished my degree in design in Mexico, New York and Paris, I decided to collaborate with my mother.

We are currently developing a clothing and lifestyle brand called *Lydia Lavín*. This project started nine years ago and today it is a nationally and internationally renowned brand. Our mission is to 'rescue' the textile traditions of our country by using fabrics and embroidery of indigenous communities in garments designed and marketed by us. The loss of the Mexican textile tradition is increasing in a vertiginous manner. Some reasons for that are the arrival of 'modernity' and mass-produced clothes in the indigenous villages, as well as the fact that a variety of situations such as marginalization and racial discrimination have led to the *Revestimiento*:[6] the use of modern clothes and the abandonment of other traditions.

As part of our work we consider our role as that of being spokespersons for this situation, but we have also taken on the task of spreading the magnificent examples of textile expertise developed throughout centuries, and promoting their study and appreciation. Similarly, we also play a part in the incorporation of these textile masterpieces in contemporary design. To us, all of these actions are very important in terms of our values, and they project us as a brand that places an importance on cultural and socially responsible fashion.[7]

Interacting with our indigenous communities

As we began to establish our fashion label we recognized that we had many obstacles to overcome, if we were to work with different indigenous community groups.

At first we found it difficult working with groups of people in remote locations, either in highlands or in an area of difficult access. We realized that this would involve travel and telecommuting. This also raised another challenge for us, which was the difficulty of language, since in many cases the artisans only speak their mother tongue or speak very little Spanish, so we have to work with interpreters. A further concern was that for indigenous groups, the notion of time is governed by daylight. They rise when the rooster crows and they end their work when the darkness of night hits; conversely, we are governed by clocks and are constantly lengthening our productive days – and we are always in a rush. Finally, we had to overcome the problem of logistics, which involved organizing the way in which we and the group would work together. We needed to organize our work patterns in such a way that it gave time for us to send supplies and for the group to send us their textiles. In particular we had to ensure that they were able to replenish the stock of parts necessary for production. At the same time, we had to overcome the difficulty of creating a market in the Mexican fashion industry which was willing to receive and support an indigenous contemporary fashion proposal.[8]

However, many things encouraged us. We were heartened to know that the different communities were so excited to work with us, and that their desire to market their work was combined with the economic need of making a living from what they do. Also, we were motivated by the interest from local and federal government bodies, who created programs that were designed to boost the production of crafts. It was also encouraging to be able to approach specific programs for innovation in crafts, as in the case of the IIDART in the state of Puebla.[9] We also discovered that there were already organized groups of artisans that had an assigned representative who acted on their behalf.

A national and international acceptance of our brand has enabled us to present it in key forums and that has been a great motivator as well. One example is the Mercedes-Benz Fashion Week in Mexico, in which we have participated over these nine years. We were also guest designers in the Fashion Week in Buenos Aires, Argentina, as well as in the *Germany's Next Topmodel* TV show, and the Congress of Fashion Group International, held in Sydney, Australia. We participated too in SIMM (the Madrid International Fashion Fair), and in 'Who's Next Paris' in January 2014. Meanwhile, the media coverage in numerous magazines and international interviews spread news of the project and endorsed the quality of our fashion products, which was helpful as a validation in our own country and helped increase the demand for our products.

But the greatest motivator for our work is the desire to conduct a transcendent community project. The project enables textile artisan communities in our country to be integrated into our contemporary design culture, creating a commercial outlet and a sustainable measure that encourages people to stay in their places of origin and produce what the area and their ancestral tradition and know-how give them. It is a project that encourages people to stay in their communities instead of searching for better life opportunities elsewhere, and thus allows them to find reasons to continue practicing their craft while taking care of their land, animals and families. It also enables the transfer of values and traditions, and provides an opportunity to reassess and revitalize the artisanal textile production they have been carrying out for thousands of years.

During these nine years we have collaborated with various indigenous and mestizo communities engaged in artisanal textile production in several states, among which we can mention our work with the Tzotzil area of Chiapas; the mestizos of Chiapa de Corzo; the Amuzgos of Oaxaca and Guerrero; and the Nahuas of the state of Mexico and in the states of Guerrero and Puebla. We have worked with the women of the Isthmus of Tehuantepec in Oaxaca and the shawl makers' centers of Tenancingo, San Luis Potosí and La Piedad, Michoacán. The experiences are varied and interesting; we are still involved in producing different products with most of the communities mentioned. In all cases we can see and confirm the benefit that the project and the assessment of their work brings to the artisans of different communities.

An example of our work

The case that most clearly explains how we work is the process of the creation of 'Mujer de la Tierra' (Woman of Earth), our autumn/winter 2013–14 collection (Figure 5.1), which was presented for the first time at the Fashion Week Mexico in April 2013. We chose to work with Hueyapan, a Nahua community in the mountain range of Puebla. We participated in a collaboration agreement between our brand and IIDART, which is a trust dedicated to the promotion of innovation through the design of crafts for the state of Puebla. The project started in January 2013 and was in full production and marketing by December 2013.

Through IIDART we were introduced to a group of Nahua women from the village who weave and embroider and are organized into a cooperative called 'Mujeres por un Sueño' ('Women for a Dream'). We had been in Hueyapan before. It is a magical village located in the northern mountains of Puebla; the climate there is very humid with plenty of rain and there is a lot of fog. The women are left alone in the community because their men migrate to work in the United States and only return to plant, harvest the fields and impregnate their wives. The work accomplished by the women is very important. They raise their children, cook food, clean the house, wash the clothes, tend the fields and take care of their animals, and are also in charge of producing their textiles and going out to sell them. It was precisely the organic textile process that the women use that inspired us to find the name that was given to the collection, 'Mujer de la Tierra' (Woman of Earth). They are women with the ability to transform what the earth gives to us into useful and beautiful things such as handcrafted textiles. The person who organizes the group and helps with translation during work sessions, Rosita Hernández, is a native of Hueyapan and a bilingual artisan. Once we talked to the people in the cooperative and the agreements were signed, we were ready to make the first working visit to Hueyapan.

First visit

We climbed up on a beautiful road surrounded by mountains covered with pepper and other fruit trees and majestic pines! We arrived at Rosita's home, which has a space adapted as a shop where they sell the products of the cooperative: shawls, wraps, blouses, scarves and bags. From there we went to the house of Doña Mary, Rosita's mother and leader of the group 'Mujeres por un Sueño'. She is a 75-year-old

Figure 5.1: Campaign for the 'Mujer de la Tierra' fall/winter 2013–14 collection.
Photographer: Juan Pablo Espinosa.

woman who has a beautiful house made of logs with a *temazcal* (an Aztec sauna) and an outside kitchen and stove. There we were offered a cup of delicious corn gruel, sweet and hot, and the rest of the women arrived, 12 in total. The atmosphere was very cheerful and we were all anxious to start working.

During the visit we were introduced to their dye process and they took us to the greenhouse, where they have all the plants from which they obtain the dye materials. We were then shown the textile process and were told how it starts: with raising the wool sheep. Once the sheep has been sheared, the wool fleece is then hit with sticks to separate the locks of hair. It is then cleaned to remove the dirt and then the fibers are spun into yarn. The women then use a waist-band loom to weave the yarn into cloth (Figure 5.2). Some pieces of cloth will remain naturally colored, while others are dyed with natural dyes derived from local

Figure 5.2: Cristina, a Nahua artisan from Hueyapan, weaving on her waist-band loom and working together with designer Lydia Lavín on samples.

Photographer: Juan Pablo Espinosa.

products: red, obtained from the cochinilla;[10] indigo blue;[11] brown, extracted from the walnut tree; yellow from the cempaxuchitl;[12] and green, extracted from plants and lichen (Figure 5.3).

Once the cloths have been woven and dyed, the women embroider beautiful patterns on them using cross-stitch, which always have specific meanings. Sometimes the meanings are very literal, such as reproductions and representations of the vegetation and wildlife of the area. At other times the meaning is more conceptual and symbolic; one example we can mention is 'the tree of life' commonly found in embroidery motifs. This is a synthetic representation of life, full of blessings and fruits; animals for abundance and fertility. It is often difficult to understand the symbolic meaning of different patterns because either the women do not know it or they do not wish to share it, since these are symbols that

Figure 5.3: Lydia Lavín working with Doña Mary on dyes.
Photographer: Juan Pablo Espinosa.

lose their magical meaning if disclosed. The designed compositions for the embroideries of Hueyapan can be 1: geometric embroideries; 2: animal and vegetable motifs; or 3: a mixture of these. Each weaver chooses how to combine their embroideries, though there are some more traditional garments that always feature the same embroidery.

At the end of the day, in the evening, we left the town but we promised to select the colors and motifs that we wanted to work with.

Second visit

Back in Mexico City, we worked on the development of the concept, the trends, color chart and sketches. The interesting thing about our projects is the achievements that are possible in the collaboration between the textile artisans and ourselves as designers, which enable us to give the best of our talent and complement one another. Learning about the work of both partners is important to the project and it provides the opportunity to exchange knowledge.

For us, it is important to learn about the techniques and traditional materials, and to analyze which ones can be adapted to contemporary garment production. We perform many tests for color resistance, durability and shrinkage. It is necessary to determine the care instructions that must be used when washing in order to preserve a garment made with indigenous textiles or embroidery. For the artisans it is important to see how their textiles can be used for purposes other than the traditional ones, and to see the new roads for marketing their products. We also support the groups with training in the development of technical specifications, so that they may work out the time and processes associated with their work, and charge appropriately based on these factors.

We went back to Hueyapan to communicate and show the group our ideas. We then placed an order for specific textiles with special dimensions and selected designs. We took some materials with us which we wanted the group to work with and we trained them in understanding the characteristics of the fabrics, which were new to the women.

The next day we worked with our crew, which included a makeup artist, Thalia Vizcarra; a photographer, Juan Pablo Espinosa; and assistants to support us as we photographed the campaign. The experience was unforgettable! Everybody participated along with us: artisans, their children, the makeup artist, the photographer and the model posing with the first samples we had prepared for the

Figure 5.4: Filomena (artisan), Lydia Lavín (designer), Dina Cores (IIDART) and Montserrat Messeguer (designer) at Filomena's shop working on the first samples we obtained from the workshops.

Photographer: Juan Pablo Espinosa.

shooting. When we returned to Mexico City we established delivery times and a timetable to organize our pattern makers and dressmaking workshop.

Third visit

A group of women from the cooperative came to Mexico City bringing the textiles we had ordered. They came also to learn about the process of dressmaking, how to prepare and interline the textiles, and they loved to see the final garments in which we have used their textiles. They enjoyed seeing our studio and the industrial processing of high fashion garments. During their visit we had meetings between the cooperative and our company involving the people responsible for logistics, payments, production and sales.

Fourth visit

We invited a group of women from Hueyapan to be at our Mercedes-Benz Fashion Week Mexico show (Figure 5.5) where we were going to launch our collection 'Mujer de la Tierra' in which they had participated.

The fashion show itself involved many people. The music was specially composed by Francesc Messeguer, my son, and produced by Eduardo Mariné, while Lorenza Luquín managed the rehearsals and choreography and the Colours Agency handled the lighting design and production. Montserrat Messeguer designed the accessories and ready-to-wear clothes, while I, Lydia, designed the cocktail garments, formalwear and eveningwear. The shoes were made in collaboration with Anukia, a Mexican footwear brand, created with the skilled artisan hands of Jalisco. The hair and makeup of the models was designed by both of us. The process of developing the sample range made in our workshop, from our initial meeting with the community group to the fashion show, took us six months. During that time we also had a fitting with the models to adjust garments, coordinated by Beatriz Calles, (director of Mexico's Fashion Week) and Laura Reyes (catwalk coordinator).

The collection consists of 26 outfits, including casual and cocktail garments, nightgowns and a wedding dress (Figure 5.6) that is the perfect ending to our work. At the end of the show we invited the group of women from Hueyapan onto the catwalk to share in the credit, receive the applause and be photographed by the press. Following the fashion show it will take us an additional five months

Figure 5.5: Runway look for 'Mujer de la Tierra' in April 2013, during the Mercedes-Benz Fashion Week Mexico.

Photographer: Juan Pablo Espinosa.

to work on the catalog of the collection and dissemination, finances, production, sales and supply to 11 boutiques where we sell the Lydia Lavín line. We have also placed a regular order for embroidery and textiles from the community so that we can maintain a constant commitment to the collaboration for the 'Cajas de Mexico' project, which involves developing accessories and corporate gifts sold under the Lydia Lavín brand.

Figure 5.6: 'Mujer de la Tierra' runway finale featuring Rosita Hernández (artisan), Doña Mary (artisan), Lydia Lavín (designer), Valeria (model), Montserrat Messeguer (designer) and Alberta Hernández (artisan).

Photographer: Juan Pablo Espinosa.

Our thoughts on the project

Since we have committed to the collaboration with the Hueyapan women, the community has created a sustainable production process which involves engaging more cooperatives to meet the textile production requirements needed for distribution. The issue of distance does not separate us, nor the consumers connected to our brand through social networks and shops.

The collaborative process has provided the community with the opportunity to continue doing what they do. Meanwhile, for us, it has opened new ways to preserve, through our designs, the traditional (and now contemporary) heritage of artisanal textiles in our country and share them with the world.

Our work has inspired other designers to work with Mexican themes, which is wonderful; but it is also a hard task for them to have in mind that an ethical approach is needed. As we have explained throughout the chapter, one has to be very respectful of the artisans' work. We have to understand that they and their work are a living history; they have been in charge of protecting and preserving their textile work and traditions, and that of course deserves to be part of any action that is considered when working with the community. As we pointed out, this has to be done in a collaborative way, which takes time, understanding and respect, as well as fair trade politics. We have seen designers go to a market place, buy a textile piece and then use it in their work without any recognition or sense of responsibility for an artisanal relationship.

In many places it is common practice for intermediaries to handle the artisan's product. The intermediaries will pay the producers a very low price and then commercialize the community and its products in the market place. They make great profits on these products and it is clear that this abusive practice is not good for the traditional textile communities. It also forces the weavers to use low quality materials so that they can work to the low prices for which their goods are bought.

Although we are working in the production of a commercial fashion brand, we do not think of it as something vain and superficial. We think of it as a responsible way of preserving the artisans' work and as an opportunity to support their practices, while we can show how to improve quality and add a value through the design of contemporary pieces. At the moment we are working on certifying our brand as 'socially responsible' through an international certification process (Worldcob Corporate Social Responsibility Certificate[13]) that requires us to meet specific demands and goals.

We are aware that many people have approached the Mexican Indian communities with political interests as well. A number of politicians flagrantly assert their support; they are photographed with artisans, and participate in interviews announcing programs and 'green and social support campaigns' that claim to help the artisans, but this is not always successful. These are some of the reasons why many people who are working with handcrafts lose confidence, and when they are approached for collaborative work it can be very hard to gain their trust.

Once respect is gained it is important to be aware of concerns that may arise when working with the communities. It can sometimes be difficult for the artisans to deliver the work as scheduled, but understanding is necessary since they may be dealing with issues arising from marginalization, poverty, poor local infrastructure, 'machismo' and climate. Our current collection was produced in the mountains of Guerrero and unfortunately the zone was devastated with heavy rainstorms, which lasted for weeks, producing great losses, for example crops, houses and roads. It took us two weeks to contact the group, who have lost everything and are still living in a camp that was established by the government to provide shelter and food. We organized a special event to gather goods, food, textile products and money to help the community rebuild their lives.

During the nine years we have been working with Mexican Indian and mestizo communities we have shared many challenging and beautiful experiences, but one thing is true: we feel fortunate that we have learned more than we have given. We have a mission and a dream to be able to preserve and collaborate with great textile masters and offer our designs to the world.

All images by Juan Pablo Espinosa: www.juanpabloespinosa.com

Notes

1 According to the *INEGI* (National Institute of Statistics and Geography) during 2012, the census reveals that there are 65 indigenous groups in Mexico.
2 Pre-Hispanic Mesoamerican cultures.
3 *Chichimeca*: ancient inhabitants of the state of Guanajuato; *Tzotzil*: ethnic group living in the state of Chiapas; *Nahua*: the *Nahuas* is a group of populations indigenous in Mesoamerica; they were the ancestors of the *Mexicas* and other ancient populations of Anáhuac, which had *náhuatl* as a common language.

4 *Instituto Nacional Indigenista* (National Indigenous Institute): decentralized organization responsible for indigenous affairs in Mexico.

5 *FONART*: Fondo Nacional para el Fomento de las Artesanías (National Fund for the Development of Arts and Crafts) is a branch of the *Secretaría de Desarrollo Social* (SEDESOL) (Secretariat of Social Development) of Mexico, which was established in 1974 to promote and protect traditional crafts.

6 *Revestimiento*: acculturation process that makes a person change their traditional attire for one that belongs to the dominant culture. It is a gradual process.

7 *Responsabilidad social empresarial (RSE) (Corporate Social Responsibility)*: defined as active and voluntary contribution by businesses to social, economic and environmental improvement.

8 *Malinchismo*: term expressing a tendency to prefer everything foreign instead of national.

9 *IIDART*: Government Fund for Boosting Innovation and Handicraft Development of the State of Puebla.

10 The cochineal is an insect that reproduces in the main rib of the nopal and from which a natural red color is extracted. The nopal or *Opuntia* is a type of plant native to the continent of America, from the Cactaceae family.

11 Indigo is a blue compound which can be made into a paste and used to dye fabrics.

12 *Cempaxuchitl*: yellow flower, a type of marigold native to Mexico.

13 www.worldcob-csr.com/en/index.php (accessed 4 July 2014).

Bibliography

Anawalt, P. Rieff (1981) *Indian Clothing before Cortés: Mesoamerican Costumes from the Codices*, Norman, OK: University of Oklahoma Press.

Lavín, L. and Balassa, G. (2001) *Museo del Traje Mexicano*, Tomos 1 al 6, México: Editorial Clío.

Loaeza, Guadalupe, Lavín, Lydia *et. al.* (2012) *Artesanía más Diseño, Puebla a la Vanguardia*, México: Editorial Trilce-IIDART.

Weitlaner-Johnson, I. (1976) *Design Motifs on Mexican Indian Textiles*, (Introduction), Graz, Austria: Akademisches Druck- und Verlagsanstalt.

PART II

FASHION FOR ENGAGEMENT

Chapter Six

fashion **People**

Participating and producing fashion

Ricarda Bigolin, RMIT University, Australia

fashion **People** is an open and inclusive model of a 'fashion house' directed by designer, RMIT lecturer and researcher Dr Ricarda Bigolin and artist and PhD candidate Adele Varcoe as part of an ongoing research project. Using the associated formats and languages of fashion design, *fashion* People investigates the way speculative and imaginative fashion products might encourage participation and social engagement. Body parts not normally 'fashioned' or sites for garments and accessories are chosen as suggestive and evocative fashion statements. The way these items encourage performance and expression and disrupt social interactions in public spaces is the intention behind the design process.

The image from *fashion* People shows a participant model being dressed for the BROW WOW WOW fashion show. This event was an informal and social approach to a fashion show, shifting the role of onlooker to that of model, changing passive viewing into active experience and contribution to fashion production. The following chapter focuses on 'participation' as a strategy for fashion practice and way to critique the production of high or luxury fashion. The project *fashion* People was initiated in a practice-based PhD project completed in 2012 at the School of Architecture and Design, College of Design and Social Context, RMIT University, Melbourne, Australia. Entitled 'Undo Fashion: Loose Garment Practice', it investigated the production and consumption of fashion by employing a range of artistic strategies involving collaborative and participatory processes. A key project within this, *fashion* People engages with the conflated identities of fashion brands and houses in their identification with a solitary designer's name, as well as the exclusiveness of high and luxury fashion. *fashion* People explores the

Figure 6.1: 2011, *fashion* People, BROW WOW WOW Bow, designed by Sanja Pahoki; dressing shot at London Fashion Colloquia.

Photograph: Panos Damaskinidis.

use of participation in fashion production; this is considered to include all the processes involved in making or manufacturing a fashion article, and also in communicating and showing fashion. Key strategies include: dispersing the design process amongst 24 different designers; the use of absurd body parts as sites for fashion articles; and viewing the fashion show as a social intervention where key 'players' in a fashion show, such as models and photographers, are randomly recruited. *fashion* People's debut collection BROW WOW WOW (the season's 'it' accessory – eyebrows!) was launched in September 2011, designed by 24 Melbourne designers and artists and modelled by the participants of Fashion Colloquia at the London College of Fashion.

Fashion and designer/house/label

Even though the designer whose name trades as a fashion house or brand is usually not the sole design entity behind an enterprise, there is still a desire to believe that the founding designer is intrinsically involved in all creations bearing such a label, from the show pieces to the sunglasses and perfumes. *fashion* People playfully explores the myth of the solitary designer namesake, thereby revealing the very collective and collaborative nature of fashion practice, not only in the large number of people involved in the creation but also in how universally precedents and models of practice are recognised. The reputation and legacy of the fashion designer is deeply folded into twentieth-century fashion history. The profession of fashion design stems from the refinement, standardisation and formalisation of systems and processes used in dressmaking and tailoring, necessary to industrialise and expand commercially.

The proposition of a collection designed for an unspecific clientele marks the emergence of the field and practice of fashion design in the nineteenth century. Prior to this, dressmakers, tailors, speciality garment makers and home sewers produced clothing (Aldrich 2003). The term 'collection' usually denotes a combination of clothes and other wearable articles 'presented together to the buying public for particular seasons' (Burns *et al.* 2011). Particular garments were sought from specialist makers (De Marly 1990) who produced custom garments through liaisons and fittings (Burns *et al.* 2011). Tailors were responsible for heavily structured garments, and dressmakers draped and decorated these structural foundations. While readily available generic or utilitarian garments are associated with ready-to-wear (or *prêt-à-porter*) practices, further advancements in this field are related to the increased profile of the fashion practitioner, symbolically in the designer label. Arguably the first example of a fashion practitioner was Charles Frederick Worth, long known as the 'father of haute couture' (De Marly 1990). Worth is recorded as being one of the first to present a collection of styles for clients to choose from and have adapted to their specific size (Troy 2003). These garments were presented in a salon environment, where a live model paraded them – a blueprint for catwalks and fashion shows. This initiated the establishment of the practice mode of *haute couture* (Burns *et al.* 2011) and Worth spurred the founding of the *Chambre Syndicale de la Confection et de la Couture pour Dames et Fillettes*, the organisation now known as the *Fédération Française de la Couture, du Prêt-à-Porter des Couturiers et des Créateurs de Mode*.

Presenting a collection of clothes on live models or mannequins, the main component of a fashion show, was a practice developed in the nineteenth century. While Worth is sometimes referred to as having pioneered this, it was arguably a practice used casually by many other parts of the fashion industry. The first cases

99

of this were when retailers or merchants had live models in the store to parade items in front of their clientele. Worth originally worked, from 1847, as a salesperson for the mercer La Maison Gagelin in Paris, where this form of casual fashion show took place (Evans 2001). When the House of Worth was founded in 1858, Worth and his wife Marie, a former model for Gagelin (De Marly 1990) appropriated this practice at his salon (Burns *et al.* 2011). This eventually developed into the presentation of collections to potential clientele on live models, at set times and for limited durations. The intention behind fashion shows has always been to promote the fashion practice or the collection. At around the time of a phenomenon for luxury and high fashion designer labels, in the 1980s, fashion houses and practitioners used the show as an opportunity to project a particular image, besides just showing or promoting the collection (Kamitsis 2009).

The designer label – or in French, *griffe* – announces the identity of a fashion practitioner. As well as marking authorship, the *griffe* establishes the design provenance of an item. This mark has a split and contradictory nature. On the one hand, it operates as the signature of the artist, a mark that gives a name to virtuosity or genius; on the other, it represents the commercial operations and enterprise involved in running a fashion house or brand:

> It signified a creative individual as well as a corporate entity, the identity of the former becoming inextricably linked to the latter, since the name of the person and that of the brand was one and the same thing.
>
> (Troy 2003: 33)

The most familiar designer labels and luxury brands are derived from the founding creator's name. In recent high fashion practices there has been a tendency to use a less specific identity by using other words, rather than the names of the creators, for their fashion house, or to use only a surname or truncated version of a name. These can still be classed as designer labels if the identity of the fashion practice is promoted and given public exposure. Kawamura explains the phenomenon of designer labels thus:

> Stars are indispensable because it is part of the ideology of creativity that creative works must have an identifiable author. Creators have their names linked to their creative product and the audience expects to know who the maker of the product is, who the creators are, who the singer and the

songwriter are, and who painted the painting. Creative production has not dissolved into the anonymity of industrial production.

(2005: 67)

The identity of practitioner, and symbolic marking on each product by way of designer label, transform the utilitarian object. The appeal of these things becomes more than their useful nature or the quality of materials or manufacture. Central to this idea is what curator Luca Marchetti describes as the 'cultural value' of fashion articles:

> The value of these objects does not derive only from the materials they are made in or the way in which they are made, but from a special relationship between those factors and the cultural significance of the context in which they are produced and received.

(2008: 43)

Many hands/many designers

In response to Marchetti's argument, as a practitioner I explore and critique fashion production processes using strategies that affect the qualities, function and value of fashion articles but also the conditions and scenarios in which these items are presented, encountered and experienced publicly. Therefore, much of my practice is concerned with opening up the fashion production process and using particular aspects of the field as sites for exploration, as discussed earlier. A notable one has been the idea of considering the fashion production process beyond just the design of products or making garments, to consider the potential and opportunities to 'design' the way people experience, interact with and use fashion. This highlights the collaborative and collective nature of 'producing' fashion and considers the multiplicity of people and skills implied by 'produce'. When the significance of this term is considered, it becomes clear that it is suggestive of a great scale of operations, formal and systematic methods, involving a large number of people, tools, machines and processes. 'Produce' implies a collaborative and resourceful approach. A producer might acquire or source things, use the skill and know-how of others and not necessarily oversee or carry out all – or any – stages of the production (Harrod 2009). In this sense producing involves many hands, many people, and the relationships between them (Petry 2011). *fashion* People intended to reveal and exaggerate this, and was initiated as a fictitious 'fashion house' that appropriated the strategies of commercial fashion practice.

In collaboration with Varcoe we set out to explore the narratives around practising as a fashion house or brand by the use of inclusive and participatory interventions and events. The aspects we explored included the ubiquity of particular roles within fashion practice, familiar languages and methods used by fashion houses, the nature of a 'collection' or the mechanics of a fashion show. *fashion* People sought playfully to expose and reconfigure these roles. In part, the intention of *fashion* People was to broach the concepts of exclusiveness in fashion that dominate various aspects of practice. We opened up the potential of a fashion house by inviting 24 local Melbourne arts and design practitioners to be the designers. This inverts the pyramid hierarchy of a fashion company, where designers and creative directors are often solitary or there are fewer individuals at the top, with numerous other staff below them.

One of the key aspects of participatory processes in creative projects is designing instructions and conditions that make participation desirable, finding ways to encourage and inspire interaction. This expands the design process, and designing begins to include all parts of communication and relationships with collaborators. Humour and playfulness are also key in getting people involved; the idea of designing a pair of eyebrows as a fashion 'must have', for example, allowed designers to be extremely imaginative. In recruiting designers for *fashion* People our strategy was to use typical fashion media jargon as well as deadpan humour that highlighted the absurdity of our requests. We asked each of the 'members' of *fashion* People to design two 'looks' for our first fashion show. The collection, entitled BROW WOW WOW (BWW), was all about 'looks for eyebrows'! We recruited members by emailing a large variety of mutual friends and peers. An extract of the email invitation follows:

> If you are up for joining us in *FASHION* PEOPLE we would ask you to:
>> Create 2 eyebrow 'looks' of any material, form or function of your choice. We would love it if these bad boys reflected your practice and the way you think about fashion. They could be quick 5-minute jobs, or extravagant masterpieces, whatever you are up for contributing!
>
> (Varcoe and Bigolin 2011)

The tone of email and graphic communication was geared at suggesting *fashion* People was an operational and functioning fashion house. A suite of 'branded' materials was developed by Simon Browne, also exploiting the idea of makeshift branding measures such as the use of round fluorescent stickers, both to form a logo and to act as a marking system for participants. Additionally, 'BWW' items were packaged in A4 plastic pockets with hooks containing a sheet with specifications about the design and a Polaroid photograph detailing how it should be worn. This echoes the management and storage of patterns, samples and specification sheets within some modes of practice. The Polaroid photograph of the practitioner wearing the 'BWW' also refers to 'back of house' procedures in fashion shows, where this image indicates to the dresser how the item should be worn.

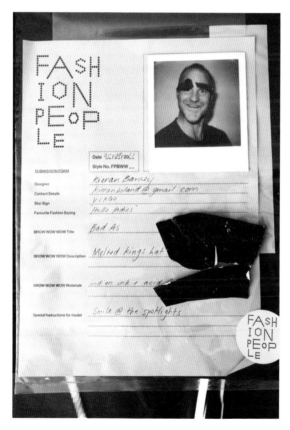

Figure 6.2: 2011, *fashion* People, BROW WOW WOW design and specification sheet.
Photograph: Panos Damaskinidis.

Due to the humorous nature of the request asking practitioners to design a pair of eyebrows, and the labelling of the fashion house as '*fashion* People', we found participation was relatively easy to encourage. Our aim was also to remove divisions between the participants and ourselves. Both Varcoe and I contributed our own 'BWW', and again we saw the design process as a way to develop methods to influence and inspire interaction. This kind of open and collective approach to designing is appealing and emphasises the way in which large fashion houses, despite being named after one designer, rarely operate with a sole practitioner entirely responsible for designing all the things produced.

BROW WOW WOW: the collection

As part of *fashion* People, we wanted to explore the way practitioners might approach the design of a body part or facial feature in the BROW WOW WOW

Figure 6.3: 2011, RAGGATT for *fashion* People, 5.30 wearing Big F*** Off Brow and Hugh Egan Westland for *fashion* People, wearing Low Brow.

collection. This opened up propositions for the development of fused categories of fashion wearables, testing the limits between garments, accessories, jewellery, cosmetics and prosthetics. These forms are not quite garments but more objects or accessories; I describe them as 'garment-like things'. This best identifies a category in which things can be worn on the body but not on areas normally associated with garments or other wearables. This type of item could use processes of fabrication taken from the fashion industry but might also start to incorporate methods from other fields, including art and beauty or cosmetic products.

In selecting a body feature – such as eyebrows – where clothing is not expected, we wanted to reflect the way fashion and beauty styles can appropriate or adopt body parts as 'it' accessories, as seen in fashion and style media (Style.com 2011). This tested how a group of different participants, some fashion-based and others art-based, would approach the design of something that is not generally part of fashion design processes. The design challenge lay in how to adhere or create a wearable pair of eyebrows, particularly with a 'wow factor' quality. This quality, when applied to brows, refers to the kind of language heard in popular fashion discourse or reality TV programmes, where ambiguous expressions such as 'wow factor' are over-used.

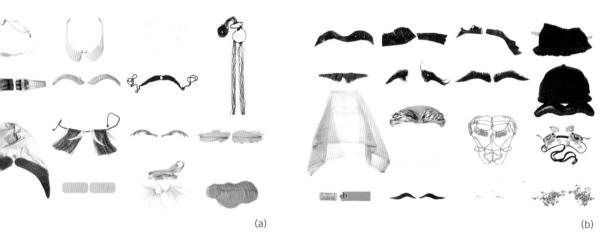

(a)   (b)

Figure 6.4: 2011, fashion People, BROW WOW WOW collection. a: Designers from left to right: Blake Barns, Busyman, Tania Spława-Neyman, Cassandra Wheat, Anna Mclaren, Créature de la Mode, Tania Spława-Neyman, Hugh Egan Westland, Cassandra Wheat, Créature de la Mode, Hannah Chamley, Joanna Henning, Busygirl, Hannah Chamley. b: Designers from left to right: Kieren Barney × 3, Madeline Stagg × 2, RAGGATT × 2, PAGEANT, Ricarda Bigolin, Simone Says, Rose Megirian, Sanja Pahoki, Ricarda Bigolin, Simon Browne, Torie Nimmervoll, Sanja Pahoki.

Photography by Linda Tegg.

Materials such as faux and real fur, human and synthetic hair, wool and sheepskin were popular choices for BWW as hairy brow extensions. These exaggerated the natural qualities of eyebrows, adding to their appearance and making them more distinct, shapely or extreme. The use of materials and techniques associated with garments created accessory-type hybrids, transposing, enlarging or revealing brows or referencing their shape. My approach was in line with the methods used in 'not really garments'. One was a piece of cotton with two neat eyebrow shapes cut out, like a simplified hijab with only eyebrows revealed; the cut-out eyebrow shapes were applied to the face with double-sided adhesive tape. Others were more noticeably accessories, such as a baseball cap with an attached padded PVC mono-brow and a scarf with supersized brows made from kangaroo hide. Scaled-down versions of garments were also popular, as were humorous hybrids such as a strappy g-string with bushy eyebrows, aprons for eyebrows and a cross between a visor and a pair of eyebrows.

Taking into account the small scale of the site, several practitioners focused on lightweight materials, ribbons and bows applied with double-sided adhesive tape. Some went in a different direction, using techniques associated with jewellery, with wires and beading as balanced or dangling adornments to brows. Another noticeable group comprised of those who opted for comic, cartoonish or caricatured eyebrows. These included scraps of paper torn into rough eyebrow shapes layered crudely in ink or stick-on polymer clay eyebrows. Some needed to be attached or applied before they could be called BWWs, such as a pair of flesh-coloured adhesive bandages for 'no-brows'; gold leaf stencilled brows applied with silicone; and a cork and lighter, which came with instructions to burn the cork and use the charcoal to draw on a mono-brow. When it is unfamiliar for a body part or site to have a garment, items become more like 'things' than garments. The process of wearing is abstracted by a lack of clear associations to body parts or definite instructions on how to wear the pieces. And also, in this case, the varied materials do not always suggest garments. While the approach used by some fashion practitioners embodied the same techniques used in garment production, others were inventing another type of body part.

The diversity of approaches indicates a whole trajectory of the categories of garment-like 'things'. Some resembled eyebrows, while others were more formless – not really eyebrows, garments or things. To enhance the 'thing-like' quality the pieces were photographed on a light box by commercial and fine art photographer Linda Tegg. We aimed to depict BWWs as a commercially viable collection, hence the rigid and ordered style of product shots, revealing details similar to those used in catalogues or for online stores.

Shifting fashion spaces

A key part of my practice has involved exploring different ways to imagine and depict 'fashion spaces' that correlate with emergent modes of practice but also take up approaches from art practice. Jessica Bugg's (2007) definition of fashion spaces as 'sites of communicating fashion' has been taken on as a point of departure, but I intended to expand the notion of what might take place within these spaces. I wanted to consider fashion spaces as more open and indeterminate, not just a place in which to watch or view the presentation of fashion as a finished object or closed performance. I aimed to use fashion spaces to present narratives about fashion, beyond being simply sites where garments or other fashion articles were on display. I considered instead how this platform could be used to generate critical ideas about fashion production and the role of practitioners. I looked for techniques to alter the dynamics of these spaces, transposing contexts; for example, design and production are assumed to take place in a site often separated from the area where fashion is viewed. Key to this is participation, which intervenes in social conditions in public spaces.

I have referred to Marchetti's (2008) notion that the value of objects or products is derived from the relationship and context of how they are produced and received. Concepts of production and consumption start to fuse, outlining interdependence and interconnections between the two. According to Miller (1987), the inevitable links that Karl Marx draws between production and consumption are that each is a logical outcome of the other. He asserts that consumption is the progression, completion and extension of production (Miller 1987: 148). Michel de Certeau defines consumption as another form of production, a way of using products that contributes to their own order of production. In this way he suggests it is what a user 'makes' or 'does' with a product (1988: xii). These ideas imply that fashion spaces might therefore entail both production and consumption.

Henri Lefebvre, in *The Production of Space*, determines the representation and construction of space by its production. Production is considered to entail a 'multiplicity of works and a great diversity of forms, even forms that do not bear the stamp of the producer or of the production process' (1991: 68). Therefore 'fashion production' could be seen as a greater network of processes used to transform the values or identities of garments and other articles through the way they are represented and experienced. This includes the production of garments and the images, performances, presentations or methods of display that influence how we read or experience these things. In line with the ideals of consumption within the context of fashion spaces, an understanding of use for fashion articles is communicated and depicted. More specific differences are in the way production is suggested to be the objective behind the processes and the nature of the site in which it takes place. Narratives about fashion processes, rituals, production and consumption are becoming features of this emergent culture of diverse fashion presentations.

The 'spectacle' quality or phenomenon of the fashion show that evolved in the last decades of the twentieth century transformed the simple process of parading clothing into elaborate and huge-scale productions. However, many fashion practices have rejected the grand-scale theatrics and associated staginess of fashion shows. This is evident in a range of inversions of the linear and elevated procession and ideology of the *défilé*. Since the late 1970s the influence of performance art has seen the stylised and regimented march of models reconfigured and relaxed by increased consideration of the performance, ritual and experience of this form of fashion presentation. The seamless and glossy façade of fashion shows enforces hierarchies and divisions in the relationships between models, audience, practitioners and the clothing on display.

BROW WOW WOW: the show

The vernacular of 'the fashion show', such as the acts of parading or being models, reveals – when used within a social context – the way fashion, and the simple act of wearing a fashion article, can influence roles and alter behaviour. The fashion show for the BROW WOW WOW collection took place during the Fashion Colloquia London, held at the London College of Fashion (LCF) in 2011. Scheduled as a pop-up event, it was to take place during a cocktail party. The atmosphere at such events can sometimes be a little reserved, and we were interested to see how the roles associated with a fashion show might be received. The idea was to recruit attendees to model or to be photographers or critics by randomly or secretly labelling them with stickers of various colours. Models were to present the eyebrow 'looks' at the cocktail party venue, and walk down a

Figure 6.5: 2011, *fashion* People, Brow Jib, designed by Ricarda Bigolin; catwalk shot at London Fashion Colloquia.

Photograph: Panos Damaskinidis.

makeshift 'catwalk' marked out with lights. Photographers were to wait at the end of the runway and capture the eyebrow looks, while the critics were to score and select their best and worst on the catwalk. Each of these roles was indicated by a different fluorescent coloured sticker given to participants in an envelope with instructions. Those for the models included a card detailing the eyebrow look they would wear and the name of the person who designed it.

A diary of the event:

> The cocktail party took place at the LCF's campus just off Oxford Street in central London. Quite a few problems arose last minute before the fashion show was to take place. The venue for the party had been moved from a more stately room with an ornate staircase that we had imagined as the perfect setting for a fashion show to the college cafeteria … This was a no-thrills room of *bains-marie*, tables, chairs and vending machines, a little outside the glamorised spaces of fashion shows. In addition, the estimated attendance was significantly lower than organisers had projected and some fashion researchers and academics weren't quite up for joining us in a FP fashion show. Luckily the charismatic Varcoe, unperturbed by some lack of interest from attendees, persisted and managed to recruit 28 models (all allocated numbered stickers), 3 photographers and 5 critics.

> I took the models 'backstage' − a meeting room a short distance from the cafeteria − whilst Adele set up the photographers and critics for the fashion show. The dressing was chaotic: 28 models in a tiny room, trying to dress themselves or each other, as well as confusion about how some of the BWW might function. I assisted some with the dressing or applying, putting the flesh-coloured 'Brow aids' (adhesive bandages) on the eyebrows of a gentleman with a distinctly darker complexion. Or by applying gold-leaf eyebrows with silicone to the forehead of a Dean of Research from LCF, who was concerned his brows weren't quite 'wow' enough. Others slipped, draped or hung on easily, and participants waited outside the cafeteria dressed and in the line-up.

> Adele was MC and announced each model and the details of their BWW, including its composition and the designer. The Sugarhill Gang's 'Rapper's Delight', an epic 14-minute rap song from the early 80s, was the chosen soundtrack. I cued and briefed the models, told them to strut and strike poses at the marked points of the catwalk. Photographers were at the end of the 'catwalk' where the models would pose numerous times. Most seemed not

too uncomfortable in the walk, or in striking poses. Gestures often emphasised or exaggerated the placement or functions of the BWWs: hands raised to eyebrows, or gesturing towards them; whilst others posed casually, naturally, as though they were perhaps not wearing any. Some were disappointed theirs weren't more dramatic, and looked enviously on at BWWs which made more impact, such as 'Brow Bling', a network of gold chains linked together, with emphasis on the eyebrows, or BWWs perceived as embodying a greater amount of labour or technique. Models were entitled to keep their BWWs after the show, and some participants were overjoyed about this. Unfortunately the BWWs that were more lo-fi, simple or conceptual constructions were often discarded or left behind after the show.

(27 September 2011)

The mixed reception of the fashion show indicated the way some attendees at this conference defined this sort of activity as unassociated with projects related to research. Most who had participated expressed belated interest in the premise of

Figure 6.6: 2011, *fashion* People: the event shot at London Fashion Colloquia.
Photograph: Panos Damaskinidis.

this event, which, for one reason or another, had lacked clear communication. It is also important to mention here that practice- or project-based research in fashion design is still a minimal area of LCF's research output. Suspicion and bemusement were a common reaction from many of the attendees when they understood this initiative was part of my PhD, conducted by project.

Despite this and the difficulties in context and audience, the photographic representations of the event taken by amateurs (along with one professional photographer) capture some of the types of behaviour and responses we were hoping to garner from participants. As BWW were 'eyebrow looks' that were in most cases easy to wear or small, it was interesting to see how a slight change in facial appearance instils ideas of masquerade and allows participants to perform or act differently from usual.

Informalising the fashion show creates a way to engage with ideals and assumptions that are often placed on this method of fashion practice. In this context, bound by certain formalities and notions of appropriate social interaction, participation in a spontaneous and informal activity was difficult to elicit and not a comfortable proposition for some. However, it was still beneficial to see how, despite the everyday surroundings of the cafeteria, participants were able to slip into roles with relative ease, emphasising the ubiquity of fashion shows. Playful inversions of these concepts are ways to intervene and change the dynamic of an event and make things like fashion shows much more open and random.

An important element is also inherent in the way this type of event reveals some particular responses towards fashion articles when they fall outside of known product categories such as beauty, clothing or accessories. These items are still considered to be more effective or more valuable if they are either dramatic or elaborate, or seem to involve greater craft or care in their production. The allure of the beautifully crafted fashion item is an undeniable and significant part of the field and is still regarded as a thing that should be displayed and presented. However, the potential and significance of fashion production also resides in the expanded ways designers present fashion, which alter our experience and understanding of fashion, and what a fashion article actually is.

References

Aldrich, W. (2003) 'The Impact of Fashion on the Cutting Practices for the Woman's Tailored Jacket 1800–1927', *Textile History*, 34 (2) pp.134–170.

Bugg, J. (2007) 'Interface: Concept and Context as Strategies for Innovative Fashion Design and Communication: An Analysis from the Perspective of the Conceptual Fashion Design Practitioner', PhD thesis, London: University of the Arts London.

Burns, L. D., Mullet, K. K. and Bryant, N. O. (2011) *The Business of Fashion: Designing, Manufacturing, and Marketing*, 4th edn, New York: Fairchild Books.

Certeau, M. de (1988) *The Practice of Everyday Life*, Berkeley, CA; London: University of California Press.

De Marly, D. (1990) *Worth: Father of Haute Couture*, 2nd edn, New York: Holmes & Meier.

Evans, C. (2001) 'The Enchanted Spectacle', *Fashion Theory*, 5 (3) pp.271–310.

Harrod, T. (2009) 'Technological Enchantment', in L. B. Newell (ed.), *Out of the Ordinary: Spectacular Craft*, London: V&A Publications.

Kamitsis, L. (2009) 'An Impressionistic History of Fashion Shows since the 1960s', in J. Brand and J. Teunissen (eds), *Fashion and Imagination: About Clothes and Art*, Arnhem, Netherlands: ArtEZ Press; Zwolle, Netherlands: d'jonge Hond.

Kawamura, Y. (2005) Fashionology: An Introduction to Fashion Studies, Oxford, New York: Berg.

Lefèbvre, H. (1991) The Production of Space, Oxford, UK, and Cambridge, MA: Blackwell.

Marchetti, L. (2008) 'Victims of Banality', in J. Brand and J. Teunissen (eds), *Fashion & Accessories*, 2nd edn, Arnhem, Netherlands: ArtEZ Press, pp.41–47.

Miller, D. (1987) *Material Culture and Mass Consumption*, Oxford, UK: Blackwell.

Petry, M. (2011) *The Art of Not Making*, London: Thames & Hudson.

Style.com (2011) 'The Look: Arch Madness', beauty trend alert. Available online at: www.style.com/beauty/thelook/112009_Eyebrows/ (accessed 2 August 2011).

Troy, N. (2003) *Couture Culture: A Study in Modern Art and Fashion*, Cambridge, MA: MIT Press.

Varcoe, A. and Bigolin, R. (2011) 'FASHION PEOPLE WANTS YOU', email to undisclosed (17 August 2011).

Chapter Seven

Open design and digital fabrication in fashion

Daijiro Mizuno, Keio University and Kyoto University Design School, Japan

Introduction

'Which would you like, beer or wine?'

Once I had a chance to interview an eminent sociologist in Tokyo on the rising popularity of digital fabrication. It was then he started talking about beer and wine. We find various branded beers in the supermarkets. They all taste differently but the quality of each respective brand is homogeneous. When it comes to wine, the quality of each bottle relies on storage, types of grape, region and the year it is produced. What the sociologist was trying to say was that we embrace digital homogeneity on one hand while celebrating analogue heterogeneity on the other. It is not either/or, we need both of them.

Perhaps we are seeing the rise of heterogeneous design generated through open design and personal fabrication. It has been considered that digital fabrication technologies are best suited for homogeneous mass production. However, with 3D printers, laser cutters, fabric printers and digital sewing and knitting machines, almost anyone can make almost anything by themselves at any given time and space. Further, bi-directional open design platforms such as Thingiverse empower the creativity of ordinary people, threatening the existing uni-directional sales channels. E-commerce services like Pinterest and Etsy suggest the presence of the user as co-creator, fostering new channels of selling, buying, manufacturing and distributing one-off goods. Digital fabrication has the potency to revolutionise the holistic consumption–production–reproduction system. While homogeneity derives from the global development of information infrastructure (internet) and machines (digital fabrication), heterogeneity derives from the *ad hoc* creative praxis that seeks for individuality. Between homogeneity and heterogeneity, the digital and the analogue, the virtual and the real and the open and the closed, we are dreaming of the potency of digital fabrication for fashion design.

This chapter is an introduction to the rising popularity of open design and digital fabrication in fashion. First, introducing the concept of open design and digital fabrication, I would like to give the general overview of what is becoming possible for emerging designers. Second, I would like to introduce two Tokyo-based fashion design brands, THEATRE PRODUCTS and Anrealage, as case studies relevant to an understanding of the implementation of open design and digital fabrication in fashion design. I argue that the future job of fashion designers is not only about designing garments to be shown on the runway under the protected licence: rather, the future designer is to act as a social agent who empowers user participation with multiple levels of customisation. With the global network of information through the internet and locally self-sufficient in terms of material needs, the task of the future designer is to design the environment in which people can make almost anything by or for themselves.

Open design and fashion

'Open design' refers to the development of physical products through the use of publicly shared information on the internet for anyone interested in making them, often performed without monetary compensation. It is no longer a mere utopian hypothesis, but has grown to be a movement that is seriously considering its potential business implementation. If open design, as the interrelation between the real and virtual communities, reconfigures the existing business model, how can fashion design reconsider the balance between what is ownable and what is shareable? This section is intended to give a brief overview on open design to explore how design can be developed by numerous stakeholders. Moreover, this is expanded later in the chapter when ideas on the modes of open design – for example collective, derivative and selective knowledge – are discussed.

A brief history of open design

The term 'open design' first appeared at the end of the twentieth century, with the founding of the Open Design Foundation. As a non-profit organisation, it set out to define open design as follows:

1   documentation of a design is available for free;
2   anyone is free to use or modify the design by changing the design documentation;
3   anyone is free to distribute the original or modified designs (for fee or for free);
4   modifications to the design must be returned to the community (if redistributed).

(Vallance *et al.* 2001: 4[1])

In reality, open design has three strands of history. One is the development of free software, renamed as 'open software' in the late 90s by Tim O'Reilly, Bruce Perens and Linus Torvalds. The second is the development of the Creative Commons licence, initiated by Lawrence Lessig in 2001, which allows a graduated copyright, between public domain and 'all rights reserved', creating new choices in reserving 'some' rights. The third strand emerged earlier and involved unnamed hardware designs, such as cutlery for 'the real world'. These were developed throughout history by anonymous (or you may say polyonymous) stakeholders. Just as characters and words can be developed, copied and modified, archetypes of open design may be derived from such design processes.

According to Bauwens (2009), there were three modes of conceiving production prior to the advent of the internet. One was the state-based system typified by that of the former Soviet Union, where the state organised production and allocated resources based on centralised planning. The second was market-based capitalism, in which the private companies control the production. Third, Bauwens describes cooperative production, in which workers or other members would own the collective capital and have some form of internal and more democratic decision-making. However, he points out that peer to peer production is different from all these production systems: it is permission-less and self-aggregated for the creation of common value (ibid.).

The wide ranging issues related to open design are discussed in *Open Design Now* (Van Abel *et al.* 2011), which is arguably one of the most important milestones in the history of the subject, as the book encompasses the vocational, legal, economic, educational, social and ethical implications of open design. The book also introduces projects ranging from 3D printers to 50-dollar prosthetic legs, suggesting how the changing roles of designers can be framed in the context of open design.

Design_Download and MAKE

When it comes to fashion specifically, there have been various attempts to make fashion 'open'. In fact, some argue that the fashion industry can be considered as a notable early adopter of open design: one can find traces of 'copied' design everywhere, but is it a good thing? Johanna Blakley, at that time Deputy Director of the Norman Lear Center at the University of Southern California, explains the benefits of being open in her TED Talk entitled 'Lessons from Fashion's Free Culture'.[2] According to Blakley, fashion design as an industry has been tolerant to derivatives of originals, to maintain its cultural dynamism. However, as the industry accelerates, such 'free' culture and open design in fashion can cause ethical, economic and legal issues, such as the fierce price competition on the high street.

Under such circumstances, SHOWstudio, a fashion website founded and directed by Nick Knight, continues to push the boundary of communicating fashion online to examine the value of the designer's work. For example, in SHOWstudio you can find the Design_Download project[3] where you can download patterns free from eminent designers including Alexander McQueen and Gareth Pugh. According to the website, the project was launched in 2002 to 'demystify the fashion process by offering prestigious designer garment patterns'. Indeed, many of the patterns available through this project are technically difficult to understand and reproduce. In this sense the project demystifies the construction of garments: it offers an aesthetic autopsy of the works of designers through an understanding of the patterns.

If SHOWstudio's Design_Download project is intended to present the creativity of designers as exclusive knowledge, *MAKE* magazine aims at the opposite: encouraging ordinary people to make and share designs between themselves as the production of collective and derivative knowledge. Published by Maker Media since 2005, this bi-monthly magazine explains how to make almost anything, in the spirit of do-it-yourself and/or do-it-with-others. While *MAKE* puts further emphasis on interactive design and design engineering, *CRAFT* magazine (which ceased publishing in 2009, although the website remains active as of June 2013[4]) should also be considered as a good example of a commons-based information sharing platform. While SHOWstudio provides the pattern in pdf format, *MAKE* and *CRAFT* magazines offer instructions. Both types of platform highlight how designers can engage with users in an innovative manner.

This section has looked at open design as the permission-less self-aggregation of knowledge, and discussed how SHOWstudio's Design_Download and *MAKE* and *CRAFT* magazines create, share and develop knowledge. In order to understand open design as 'design with others', Figure 7.1 clarifies these differing modes as:

1   collective knowledge production as a form of mass-collaboration;
2   selective knowledge production as seen in the natural selection process;
3   derivative knowledge production with infinite variants of the archetype.

Open design is changing the relationship between designers, clients and users: the designed outcomes are not necessarily exact, finished and tangible. The design is not necessarily completed by a designer; it can be left open to its users to generate variants of their own.[5]

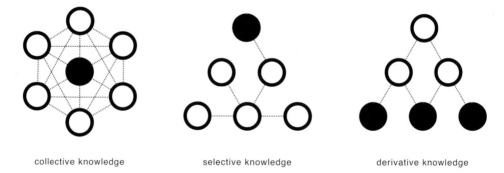

collective knowledge   selective knowledge   derivative knowledge

Figure 7.1: Collective, selective and derivative knowledge production.

Digital fabrication and fashion

Neil Gershenfeld, the originator of the Fab Lab at the Center for Bits and Atoms at Massachusetts Institute of Technology, wrote in *Fab* (2007) that digital fabrication will empower users to engage in making almost anything. On the other hand, Chris Anderson, a former *Wired* magazine US Editor-in-Chief, indicated in *Makers* (2012) that digital fabrication technology will turn the existing industrial structure upside down, giving more power to the individual entrepreneurs. As the technology allows almost anyone to print out information as tangible atoms, niche demands and the ideas of the novice user are becoming more visible in the public space. However, what is the implication of digital fabrication in the fashion industry? The following section offers a brief overview of digital fabrication technology and explains how it can have an impact on various levels of manufacturing.

The advent of digital fabrication

Digital fabrication is a manufacturing process that involves the use of computer software programs to construct objects. Machines operated by Computer Numerical Control (CNC), initially developed for industrial manufacturing processes, use numerics to control the speed, velocity and position of machining heads to manipulate objects. As the basic patents relating to additive manufacturing, owned by 3D printer manufacturer Stratasys, expired in 2009, the price of 3D printers has dropped significantly from several thousand pounds to just hundreds for personal desktop fabrication.

However, CNC machines, or digital fabrication, are not merely about 3D printing; they can be both additive and subtractive. In the fashion industry, digital fabrication has been applied to various manufacturing processes including laser cutting, knitting, weaving, sewing and embroidery. In particular, embroidery machines have been developed for various procedures including satin stitch, chain stitch, sewing on of sequins, appliqué and cutwork. In order to mass produce fabrics, computer-controlled multi-sewing head embroidery machines were introduced by the Japanese company Barudan in 1977, while the US company Wilcom introduced the embroidery design system to run on a computer in 1980. Since then, numerous companies have developed various machines and software to operate computer-controlled embroidery for various scales of manufacturing (Schneider 2011).

Perhaps due to the range of finishing, styles and size, there has been much confusion about which machine formats (hardware) and source formats (software) are best suited to make the desired embroidery. One needs to know how to design and make the data while converting one format to the other. Although the advent of the embroidery machine is only one aspect of digital fabrication in the fashion industry, the task for the future designer is to grasp the potency of digital fabrication technology in the broader perspective. This includes:

1   TRANSLOCAL
    Digital fabrication can empower site-specific projects with locally available techniques and materials, combined with digital data accessible on the internet.
2   TRANSHISTORICAL
    Digital fabrication can revitalise and reproduce old products from any given moment in time. Once they are created and archived as digital data they can be treated like any other archived material, giving more opportunities for potential re-use.
3   TRANSFORMAL
    Since tooling lead time is far shorter than in manual manufacturing, digital fabrication can allow designers to produce many variants. Additionally, emerging design fields such as parametric design and algorithm design fall into this category.

Personal fabrication and mass customisation

Gershenfeld wrote in *Fab* (2007) that the analogy between the personalisation of fabrication and that of computation is close and instructive. If Gershenfeld is right, one can relate the birth of the personal fabricator to the history of the personal computer. As introduced in *A Computer Perspective* (Eames 1973), one of the origins of the computer can be found in the 1940s, when ballistics and breaking cryptic codes were of great importance, after which more commercial use followed, such as the calculation of payslips. In 1976, the Apple 1 – a legendary 'wooden case' personal computer – was produced by the Apple Computer Company and revolutionised our perception of the computer. The personal computer was still expensive, but Steve Jobs and Steve Wozniak were foreseeing our future life through the personalisation of computers. We all know what happened to Apple after that, and perhaps the 3D printers that we see now are the modern equivalent of the Apple 1.[6]

Personal fabrication is, in other words, the democratisation of digital fabrication technology to empower the creativity of ordinary people. This is the paradigm shift from 'mass production to mass customisation' for the manufacturing business. The concept of mass customisation emerged in the late 80s, offering customisable products and services in a competitive and segmented market. According to Da Silveira *et al.*, there are five levels of mass customisation strategies:

1   Pure Standardisation (suited for large corporations)
2   Segmented Standardisation (suited for medium–large corporations)
3   Customised Standardisation (suited for small corporations)
4   Tailored Customisation (suited for entrepreneurs)
5   Pure Customisation (suited for any individuals).

(2001)

As users take charge of design, they can become 'consumer' as well as 'producer'. However, while the digital fabrication technology empowers the creativity of ordinary people, some may be excluded from this service. Democratising fabrication is a wonderful idea, but users need to be able to choose the right level of participation. In response to the classification above, Stappers *et al.* (2011) comment on the changing relationship between the client, user and designer and suggest there are multiple layers of user participation and differing designer tasks. Designers have to work with users by handing over different areas of their authority, as it were, giving them help in their activities in ways such as prescribing (where the designer acts like a doctor, prescribing a design for each person); menu (the designer, like a chef, offers sets of designs for each person to choose from); co-creation (the designer works with the person); and DIY assistance (the designer acts as a facilitator and gives support). Da Silveira *et al.* outline six factors needed for successful mass customisation systems:

1   *Demand of the users*
    The presence of increasing user demand for customisable products is evident, though research should be conducted to understand what level he/she wants to be involved in the process of making.
2   *Timing of development*
    Mass-customisable design depends on the readiness of the user community. It may require training/education prior to the implementation of mass customi-sation service.

3   *Value chain readiness*
    The supply network should be at close proximity to deliver materials quickly while it should also be networked globally. Creating self–sufficient and self–resilient maker communities can revitalise the notion of locality.

4   *Information technology*
    It is up to designers and engineers to figure out how the advanced manufacturing technologies can be translated into the everyday practice of users: free online softwares are one of the examples on fostering user community.

5   *Product customisability*
    Creating independent modules that can be assembled into different forms. In the fashion industry this is closely related to the notion of extending product lifecycle as users reshape the modules.

6   *Knowledge exchange platform*
    Fostering the culture of DIY or DIWO (Do It With Others). There has to be a place where ideas are freely exchanged and distributed.

(2001)

Designing a movement with the concept that almost anyone can make almost anything requires the integration of the infrastructure (internet, software and hardware availability) and the superstructure (culture of user community). Rather than (futile) competition between the large scale manufacturers and the independent designers, exploring services for differing levels of user participation should be encouraged. Designers are then not only making garments for anonymous buyers; instead they are engaging with local/global communities.

Manufacturers	Machines	Levels of Customisation
large corporation	£100,000	standardisation
small corporation	£10,000	modular production
mature maker	£1,000	customised service
amateur maker	£100	self design

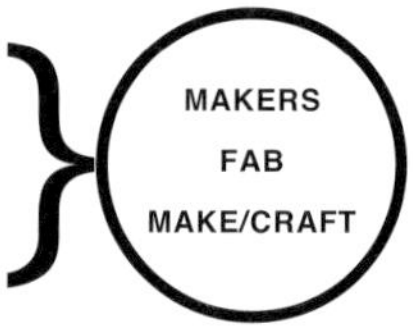

} MAKERS
  FAB
  MAKE/CRAFT

Figure 7.2: Roles of manufacturers and machines in relation to the level of mass customisation.

To date the chapter has introduced digital fabrication and explored levels of mass customisation for user participation in personal fabrication. To clarify the discussion Figure 7.2 represents the new domains in fashion design, which include:

1   *Designing prescribed standards*
    Professional machines and material production for making standards. Innovation at this level is best suited to large corporations as it deals with multiple stakeholders.
2   *Designing customisable processes*
    Semi-professional machines and materials for modular production, supporting the respective needs of individual user. It can be best performed by small corporations and mature makers.
3   *Designing garments together*
    Household machines for personal fabrication as open design, with no monetary compensation.

If garments are designed to provide adaptability then the designer has to create a holistic environment that entrusts a number of design choices to the user, as co–creator. As a 'meta-designer' who redesigns design, the designer now becomes someone who designs the environment, system, service, method, module and database for designers.

Case studies: THEATRE PRODUCTS and Anrealage

THEATRE PRODUCTS and 'THEATRE, yours' 00

THEATRE PRODUCTS is a Tokyo-based fashion brand founded in 2001 by a creative producer, Kao Kanamori, and two designers, Akira Takeuchi and Tayuka Nakanishi. In 2012, at the design symposium DESIGNEAST, the brand launched 'THEATRE, yours' 00, a workshop/exhibition that encouraged user involvement in the design process. At the workshop participants could choose desirable patterns and fabrics designed by THEATRE PRODUCTS to make into garments at the site. After completion, the finished garments were photographed and the results were shown on the official THEATRE PRODUCTS website.[7] By defining and experiencing the design process, the participants understood the time and effort needed to make a garment and therefore they re-acknowledged the value.

Figure 7.3: 'THEATRE, yours' 00 workshop ©THEATRE PRODUCTS.
Photograph: Mai Narita.

THEATRE PRODUCTS then sold the patterns for non-commercial use with a Creative Commons licence so that participants could customise them freely after the workshop session.

'THEATRE, yours' workshop store

Following the success of the workshop, in 2013 THEATRE PRODUCTS launched 'THEATRE, yours' workshop store so that people could experience the 'THEATRE, yours' 00 workshop online.[8] The online workshop begins by choosing a garment, followed by a process of customisation using a selection of haberdashery items, and then the order is placed. Previously designed and finished garments from other participants are uploaded on the official website. The 'THEATRE, yours' workshop store is a unique example of mass customisation initiated by a fashion brand that works on encouraging collective knowledge by sharing results on the internet. The online workshop can enrich the experience of the fan-based community that lives in both the virtual and the physical space.

Figure 7.4: 'THEATRE, yours' 00 workshop at DESIGNEAST03.
Photograph: Daijiro Mizuno.

Users can learn to create fashion by sharing knowledge between members of the community while strengthening the social bonds between users and designers.

Anrealage

Kunihiko Morinaga, a founder of Anrealage, was first known for the use of meticulous and intricate patchwork in his design work. Subsequently it was his 2009 collection that became widely known as he interrogated the relationship between the body and the garment. Making garments based on 3D shapes, including the sphere-, pyramid- and box-shaped bodice, he questioned the correlation between the enveloping and the enveloped. Since then, Morinaga has been working with modellers called Mudsnail to explore the potential use of 3D computer-aided design (CAD) programs such as Rhinoceros, and digital fabrication in fashion design.

Wideshortslimlong

For his 2010–11 Autumn/Winter collection, Morinaga showcased a collection entitled Wideshortslimlong. For this collection, he worked with a wide-short body and a slim-long body, made using 3D CAD technology. The wide-short pieces distort the height by 250 per cent (width) and 70 per cent (length), while the slim-long garments distort by 80 per cent (width) and 150 per cent (length). The use of 3D CAD enabled Morinaga to make protoypes rapidly on the desktop, thus reducing risk and cost. It was by designing through 3D CAD that Morinaga came to observe the body as a sculptable object with which to explore new enveloping garments.

Time

Morinaga employed Viscotecs, a digital fabric printing service for mass customisation offered by Seiren[9] for the 2012–13 Autumn/Winter collection. Seiren has created

Figure 7.5: 2010–11 Autumn/Winter collection: Wideshortslimlong ©Anrealage.
Photograph: Seiji Ishigaki (Blockbuster).

Figure 7.6: 2012–13 Autumn/Winter collection: Time ©Anrealage.
Photograph: Seiji Ishigaki (Blockbuster).

a service using a digital fabric printer, which allows the designer to order small print jobs quickly and efficiently. Prior to the advent of digital fabric printing, designers had to work with screen printing services that required a lead time of few months before manufacturing. Understanding the merits of digital fabric printing, Anrealage played with design software programs such as Photoshop and Adobe Illustrator to reflect the notion of movement in time using blurred images or prints, while also experimenting with garment shapes that reacted against the movement of the body.

Bone

For this collection, Anrealage worked on the recognition of garments in space. Taking off the outer 'flesh' of the garment, Morinaga tried to explore the fundamentals of clothing with the notion of 'bones', using laser cutting to form narrowly cut garments that revealed a mapping of the body. Using materials like neoprene, the garments were cut at a high temperature so that the raw edges were 'melted' and finished neatly.

Figure 7.7: 2013 Spring/Summer collection: Bone ©Anrealage.
Photograph: Seiji Ishigaki (Blockbuster).

Summary

THEATRE PRODUCTS shows us how a designer brand can co-create garments with users using a process of democratisation that gives away the power of designing to the user. Furthermore it is also suggested that the use of a Creative Commons licence, in the context of mass customisation, can change the relationship between designers and users. It is in this context that THEATRE PRODUCTS has tried to foster creativity between multiple stakeholders. On the other hand, Anrealage explores commercially viable design developed using digital fabrication technologies, and pushes the boundaries of manufacturing processes available to the designer. Digital fabrication in the context of personal fabrication can serve as a great aid for small scale, unique and highly original garment production.

Discussion: the future of fashion design for a sustainable society

This chapter has looked at open design and digital fabrication and sketched out the task ahead for future fashion designers, who may act as meta–designers empowering the creativity of ordinary people. However, there are a number of points that need to be considered. First, Laitio (2011) argues whether open design can contribute to the world's bigger problems, such as the depletion and squandering of natural resources, population growth, consumerism and widespread poverty. In turn he suggests that we should question whether the pooling of knowledge and resources, the re-evaluation of the concept of time (in terms of the production process and the use of fashion) and the facilitation of user participation can help open design make a strong contribution to sustainability (Laitio 2011: 191).

Through the internet there is the potential for anyone to become an open designer and this marks a need for new relationships to be forged between companies, capitalists, designers and users. However, in respect of this paradigm shift, one question is: should this new system be dependent on self-organisation just like the eco-system of the internet? Permission-less self-aggregation of knowledge for/with/by those who make a living through sharing may be idealistic, but it will require new and different legal systems to allow people to use the available data, with or without monetary compensation. The Creative Commons licence is a good initiative, but can it also be applicable to the embodied information?

How can we create the sustainable 'consumption' of knowledge and materials? To answer this, meta-designers will have to identify what can be sold, purchased and shared. It is in this context that the service design for open design must be developed, to provide a platform where people have access to necessary resources free or for a fee, through the use of established levels of user participation. This may appear to reflect existing online sales platforms, but as the data becomes tangible (a product in itself) it requires the intersection of a virtual and physical platform. Thus the role of social agents like Fab Labs, local corner shops or tailors that contribute to the local economy should be reconsidered as the technology facilitates both homogeneity and heterogeneity in economy and manufacturing. De Mul (2011) indicates that designers should not abandon their activities as designers; rather, they should redesign the activities themselves. The designer of the future has to become a database designer, a meta-designer, not designing objects, but shaping environments in which unskilled users can access and design their own objects.

But if everyone becomes a designer, how do we value design? The critique of open design will become one of the important elements to sustain design as culture. While communication platforms that are based on collective, selective and derivative knowledge should be encouraged, we also need to ask how we determine the ethical correctness of the available data. For example, the Wiki Weapon Project was highly instructive in that it alerted us to what becomes possible in the age of digital fabrication; giving away free data to manufacture guns with 3D printers is an ethical and political issue.

If this approach is appropriate, what is the vocational specification of the future designer as meta-designer? Is he/she an educator, architect, lawyer or manager? We need to begin to articulate and define the integrated tasks of the meta-designer. In between homogeneity and heterogeneity, the digital and the analogue, the virtual and the real, and the open and the closed, meta-designers will have to work out new methods of design. Open design and digital fabrication can enrich and enhance our lives, but through working with polyonymous stakeholders the task for emerging fashion designers will be to explore how much derivative knowledge one can foster and harvest. If polyonymous creativity creates new eco-systems, as evidenced in fashion, then this may determine what and how fashion designers develop in the future.

Notes

1 Some descriptions of open design to be found on the P2P Foundation's website are: 'design whose creators allow it to be freely distributed and documented and condone modifications and derivations of it'; 'CAD information published online under a CC license to be downloaded, produced, copied and modified. An Open Design is produced directly from file by CNC and without special tooling'; and 'a new economic model for design that distributes power among creative professionals and local manufacturers, rather [than] concentrating it in centralized industrial brands'. Available at: http://p2pfoundation.net/Open_Design (uploaded on 18 May 2006) (accessed 4 July 2014).

2 www.ted.com/talks/johanna_blakley_lessons_from_fashion_s_free_culture.html (accessed 4 July 2014).

3 http://showstudio.com/project/design_download (accessed 4 July 2014)

4 http://makezine.com/craftzine/ (accessed 4 July 2014).

5 A great example of an open design project can be found in product design: *Autoprogettazione?* (Mari 2002), a catalogue of Enzo Mari's 1974 project, provided open source instructions for making wooden furniture. By selling instructions, he questioned consumerism and the social responsibility of a designer. Autoprogettazione continues today as a great expression of open and collaborative design made topical by digital technologies, creating numerous derivatives of the original projects:
'Autoprogettazione Revisited' Exhibition at Architectural Association School of Architecture London (AA School): www.aaschool.ac.uk/Downloads/Autoprogettazione_Revisited_instructions_web.pdf (accessed 4 July 2014); Autoprogettazione 2.0 at FabLab Torino: www.domusweb.it/en/news/2012/04/11/autoprogettazione-2-0-on-display.html (accessed 4 July 2014); Kagu-No-Katagami (patterns for furniture) Fab Commons downloadable furniture as (derivatives of the originals by MUJI): www.muji.net/lab/ateliermuji/exhibition/121026-katagami.html (accessed 4 July 2014).

6 When it comes to fashion the first 'computational' machine is said to be the introduction of punched cards for textile looms by Joseph Marie Jacquard in 1801 (Eames 1973). Known for Jacquard weave, it was the first attempt to programme design that is incorporated into a woven structure rather than dyed or printed.

7 http://theatreyours.tumblr.com/ (accessed 4 July 2014).

8 http://theatreyours-wss.com/ (accessed 4 July 2014).

9 www.viscotecs.com/english/index.html (accessed 4 July 2014).

Bibliography

Anderson, C. (2012). *Makers: The New Industrial Revolution*, London: Random House

Anrealage (2013). *A REAL UN REAL AGE*. Tokyo: Parco Publishing

Ashida, H. and Mizuno, D. (2012). *Fashionista*, 001, Fashionista Editorial

Ashida, H. and Mizuno, D. (2013). *Vanitas*, 002, Vanitas Editorial

Bauwens, M. (2009). The Emergence of Open Design and Open Manufacturing. Available online at: www.we-magazine.net/we-volume-02/the-emergence-of-open-design-and-open-manufacturing/#.UbHIoPax60g (accessed 19 February 2009)

Da Silveira, G., Borenstein, D. and Fogliatto, F. S. (2001). Mass Customization: Literature Review and Research Directions, *International Journal of Production Economics*, 72(1), pp. 1–13

De Mul, J. (2011). Redesigning Design, in Van Abel, B., Evers, L., Klaassen, R. and Troxler, P. (eds), *Open Design Now*. Amsterdam: BIS Publishing, pp. 36–37

Eames, C. and Eames, R. (1973). *A Computer Perspective: Background to the Computer Age*, Cambridge, MA: Harvard University Press

Gershenfeld, N. (2007). *Fab: The Coming Revolution on Your Desktop – from Personal Computers to Personal Fabrication*, New York: Basic Books

Ghalim, A. (2013). Fabbing Practices – an Ethnography in Fab Lab Amsterdam, thesis, Amsterdam: New Media and Culture Studies, University of Amsterdam

Kadushin, R. (2010). Open Design Manifesto. Available online at: www.ronen-kadushin.com/files/4613/4530/1263/Open_Design_Manifesto-Ronen_Kadushin_.pdf (accessed September 2010)

Laitio,T. (2011). From Best Design to Just Design, in Van Abel, B., Evers, L., Klaassen, R. and Troxler, P. (eds), *Open Design Now*. Amsterdam: BIS Publishing, pp. 190–198

Mari, E. (2002). *Autoprogettazione?* Ediz. italiana e inglese, Milan: Corraini

Schneider, D. K. (2011). Computerized Embroidery. Available online at: http://edutechwiki.unige.ch/en/Computerized_embroidery (accessed 4 April 2011)

Sinclair, C. (2008). *Craft: Transforming Traditional Crafts: the 2nd year*, box set, volumes 5–8, Maker Media

Stappers, P. J., Visser, F. S. and Kistemaker, S. (2011). Creation & Co: User Participation in Design, in Van Abel, B., Evers, L., Klaassen, R. and Troxler, P. (eds), *Open Design Now*. Amsterdam: BIS Publishing

Tanaka, H. (2012). *Fab Life*, Japan: O'Reilly Japan

Tapscott, D. and Williams, A. D. (2008). *Wikinomics: How Mass Collaboration Changes Everything*, London: Penguin

Vallance, R., Kiani, S. and Nayfeh, S. (2001). Open Design of Manufacturing Equipment, in Proceedings of the CHIRP 1st International Conference on Agile, Reconfigurable Manufacturing, Council for Health Improvement through Research and Practice (CHIRP International)

Van Abel, B., Evers, L., Klaassen, R. and Troxler, P. (eds) (2011). *Open Design Now*, Amsterdam: BIS Publishing

Chapter Eight

Form empowered by touch, movement, and emotion

Eunjeong Jeon, Curtin University, Western Australia

A great many of our emotions, and in particular comfort, can be evoked by our experience of movement during everyday activities, for example touching, wrapping, and walking. This is because our perception of emotion is drawn from how our bodies experience or interact with the world, whether in the form of objects, living beings, situations, or events, intermingled with sensory experience and action (Merleau-Ponty 1962). It is argued that the quality of these movements can inform and steer design practice towards an emotion- and sensorimotor-driven approach in fashion design, since it provides a rich source of stimuli for the creation of new garment forms that establish the body as a primary source and an essential structure from which to understand the nature of bodily interaction.

This chapter presents two case studies from the research project entitled 'Form Empowered by Touch, Movement, and Emotion',[1] which draws on the nature of experiential bodily knowing and understanding that is generated through the phenomenological way people touch, move, and feel in the process of interacting with an object. By 'researching-through-design' the project aimed to contribute to the discourse on comfort in clothing by investigating the influence of tactile (haptic) experience, kinaesthetic interaction, and emotion. The investigation expands the knowledge of design practice by focusing on how a garment empowers the body to touch, feel, and move in order to enhance self-expression and self-therapy. In this sense the garment is an interactive object that can contribute in the development of new design ideas by opening a new space for users. Garments can be created with users or even by users, 'designing experience or interactions' in relation to their need for comfort in an everyday living environment.

Feeling through touching, seeing through touching

Touching is an important way of exploring our senses and emotions since it can help us understand an object's aesthetics and dimensions of comfort. We can experience a feeling of comfort based on what we see an object through, what we touch, and how we touch. For example, when you touch an old, soft, fluffy woollen blanket that has absorbed the scent of your body, it invites you to stroke the surface with your hands or wrap it around your body to create a cocoon. Through the touching process, the blanket evokes not only sensorial experiences, such as smoothness and warmth, but also sensuous imagery, such as empathy and nostalgia. This is what Merleau-Ponty elucidates when establishing a sensory experience: 'the senses intermingle and mutually resonate' (1962: 229–230). His philosophical idea stresses unity of tactile and kinaesthetic phenomena, and unity of senses. In other words, this theory indicates that, for example, there is a close link between the perceived object and the person perceiving it. We are able to 'see' an object sensuously and perceptually through the hand's touch; the hand is a perceptual and manipulative organ that connects with the entire body (Gibson 1966). In addition, perceiving sense through action (touch and movement) is a reciprocal system. We feel comfortable intuitively through touch and through the way our body moves or is moved by finding our own individual levels of comfort. This perspective is significant for the design of body-centred and sense-driven clothing, especially when the intertwining of senses and motor skills enhances our emotions.

The research-through-design approach, *feeling through touching, seeing through touching*, explores how a methodology of tactile (haptic) experimentation, which is intertwined with feeling, touching, and seeing, could influence the design process to create communicable knowledge through the act of designing. Haptic experimentation through body empowerment makes people (including designers) more creatively active (Deleuze 2003). This is because our body is experienced as a duality, both as an object (for example you can touch your own hand) and as your own subjectivity (for example you can feel something by touching with the hand, and hand touching can have an influence on how you feel something on your body). Thereafter you can experience being touched. Moreover, imagination can be used to fill in the missing components of a conscious image; however, this is not through thought but rather through action. This action-driven haptic interface has a powerful influence on people's strong sensuous response.

Accordingly, in designing garments it is necessary to measure the degree of comfort that is experienced by the user during bodily interaction. This approach to designing garments draws on the user's act in doing, rather than thinking.

Research process

The design explorations were carried out in an experiential manner through a process of action and reflection. The focus of the project concentrated on the haptic experience of women (n=15, ages 20–40), particularly on their responses to how they touch and move; what they feel through touch; how and what they see through touch and how this affects their thinking; and how touching by hand relates to the touching of other parts of the body.

Four important outcomes, which influenced the textile design, resulted from the observations of the participants. First, various emotions were evoked by the way participants handled the fabric, for example stroking, squeezing, rubbing, lifting, sliding, and pressing. Most of the participants easily experienced passive touch, such as sliding, pressing, and fumbling. However, when the participants exerted an active touch, such as stroking, squeezing, pressing, and lifting, they seemed to engage in a more sensory experience (Figure 8.1).

Using an active touch, in particular to squeeze and compress the surface (detected texture) of the textiles using the five fingers of the hand, enhanced the strongest bodily sensory–tactile experience for 'feeling good' and also, paradoxically, 'feeling bad'. Second, it was revealed that unconscious movements – in this case, how participants played with an object without thinking – seemed to influence positive affective states. For example, unconscious gestures such as pressing and rolling seemed to make the participants calm, soothing their state of discomfort, anger, or annoyance. In the experiment, it became apparent that such unconscious movements could assist people to evoke positive emotions, or could alter their negative states by bringing on positive emotions, moods or sentiments. Third, the results showed that active hand touches were related to how this body part is sensorially intertwined. This is because the process of obtaining a sensory experience from hand touching was coordinated with whole body movements. Therefore this contributed to the overall impression of feeling 'good' or 'bad'. Finally, it was revealed that sensory modalities were connected perceptually. For example, when participants touched an object whilst blindfolded, they described their conscious images as evoking 'ripples in

Figure 8.1: Categories of modes of movement: 15 participants were observed for dynamic touches: stroking, grabbing, fumbling, pressing, rolling, sliding, rubbing, and squeezing.

water = soft = surface = feeling good'. The results revealed that what participants touched affected what they saw.

Design approach

The project 'Touch me, Feel me, Play with me' stems from a reflection on the outcomes of the haptic experiments discussed earlier, and the philosophical concept of phenomenology. The primary research question was: how can textiles empower the body to touch/be touched, feel/be felt, and move/be moved to enhance self-expression and self-therapy?

In order to explore the question, the process of design involved a twofold approach: haptic touching and haptic seeing (Craig and Rollman 1999). In the context of haptic touching, the textile is designed to invite the wearer to create

Figure 8.2: Structure of 'Touch me, Feel me, Play with me': on the one side, an irregular polygon, shaped with both concave and convex forms, is a trapped air structure. On the reverse side, geometric pockets are created.

dynamic modes of touch. Different modes of touch stimulate different levels of sensorial responses (Figure 8.1). The felted wool textile was developed in consideration of these dynamic touches and was structured to incorporate an irregular polygon, shaped with both concave and convex forms, to trap air on one side and create geometric pockets on the reverse side (Figure 8.2). This 3D structure expands as different points of body come into contact with the skin, stimulating and enhancing a sensorial experience. Felted wool is used for the material explorations because it has innate properties such as resilience, versatility, and roughness but still creates soothing and warm feelings. The quality of the textile is also designed to be open to diverse experiences. For this reason, the textile can be configured in various ways through different bodily interactions, allowing the wearer to express individuality. Therefore the body itself becomes an essential structure in crafting the form of the textile design (Figure 8.3).

Figure 8.3: 'Touch me, Feel me, Play with me' garment: different inside and outside textures and forms allow the wearer to elicit various sensorial experiences, which enhance dynamic self-expression.

Photographer: Kyunghoon Kim.

In the context of haptic seeing, the textile design is focused on texture and crafting. 'Touch me, Feel me, Play with me' is produced using crafting techniques such as sewing, folding, and engineered felting (Figure 8.3). Craft techniques are used in the making of the textiles so that they project a sophisticated aesthetic while maintaining a soft texture. In addition, the textile is designed to enhance personal tactility by encouraging the wearer to move over and interact with the textile surface. The wearer is able to engage with the textiles to make her own form through craft techniques and become involved in the creative process, as a way to stimulate an interpersonal dialogue between wearer and garment. This dialogue can lead the wearer to develop an attachment to the garment since personal stories become embedded in the prototype. Therefore, the wearer can experience a variety of feelings and emotions while interacting with or without the textile form.

Doing through feeling, feeling through doing

The human body is designed for movement. The movement expresses human emotions and creates a particular bodily orientation and experience in response to the world the body inhabits. When I attended a workshop entitled 'Fremantle on the Edge', in Western Australia in 2009, I was able to engage in an active experiment of body interaction with nature through sand, water, shadow, and movement. The aim of the experiment was to explore spontaneous feelings in a natural environment using the conscious or unconscious bodily knowing process, which was a crucial method for developing the concepts in the early phase of the design process. Rather like the form that is created in nature, which continuously evolves through the perpetual phenomenon of growth in time and space, the empowerment of form through bodily movement (i.e. hugging, holding, and embracing the water) continuously evolves to bring meaning and sense to our everyday, embodied experience of space. In this sense form is indefinite and imperfect but it is ongoing, as it transforms from one form into another in relation to a space where the body perceives sense and emotion. Reflecting on this active bodily experiment with nature I was curious to explore further how a garment can encourage people to feel and move, and configure their own level of comfort, in different emotional states and living environments.

Research process

The research-through-design approach applied in *doing through feeling, feeling through doing*, intended to investigate how meaningful bodily expressive actions are manifested in emotional experiences (for example happiness and fear) while interacting with a garment. The study involved observing a group of women engaging in a series of choreographic interactions as a way of exploring behaviour and performance in relation to different forms of garment.

The first phase of the interactive choreographic study explored 'emotionally expressive action with the garment' to understand the emotive movement of women (n=15, ages 20–40), and in particular how they interact with a garment to transform their feelings of fear into a recognizable state of comfort; and how they interact with a garment to reinforce their feeling of pleasure as a recognizable state of comfort. This part of the study sought to understand the dynamic expressiveness of bodily behaviour, and the satisfaction and comfort experienced by women when they formed and configured the garment for their body using a process of wrapping. A key outcome of the study was the revelation that, when wearing clothing in the emotional context of comfort, the participants used their clothing to wrap or hold their body, both for the purpose of protecting, hiding, and disguising themselves in insecure situations (that is, to evoke feelings of relief and security) and for self-expression in secure situations (that is, to express feelings of pleasure and enjoyment). In addition, it is also important to point out that the emotion experienced by the women tended to change within an interactive wrapping process.

The second phase of the study involved observing the characteristics of bodily movements of women (n=8, ages 20–40), such as body positions, attitude, shapes, and movement patterns of their head, hands, legs, and trunk, in a comparative study of different walking styles ('natural', 'happy', and 'fearful') and garment styles ('normal', 'happy', and, 'fearful'). The study, using both scientific motion capture data analysis and Laban Movement Analysis (Laban 1960), provided a range of observations and understandings of the moving body in the context of the emotional experiences of, and garments worn by, the participants.

More specifically, 3D motion capture data was used to collect and analyse the various head, hand, and leg movements of a participant when interacting with a garment, in different emotional scenarios (Figure 8.4). The observations were focused on a range of body movements, such as side-to-side, up–down, forward–backward, in the context of different garment styles and different emotions; the velocity of motion while wearing each garment style; and ways of stepping. In the observations, three walking types revealed significantly different bodily movements, showing that these can be affected not only by specific emotions but also by specific garment types. For example, the happier that a participant felt, the more the head moved up–down and the hands moved from side to side, up–down, and forward–backward. When a participant became fearful, the head moved in a side-to-side motion. When a participant wore the 'normal garment' the hands swung

Figure 8.4: 3D motion capture image: example of the 'fearful walk' trial, where a person performed while interacting with the 'fearful garment'.

noticeably more, and faster, in a side-to-side, up–down, and forward–backward motion. This expression was much more pronounced than it was with the other garment styles, including the 'happy garment' and the 'fearful garment'.

The Laban (1960) Movement Analysis (LMA) – Body, Space, Shape, and Effort – was used to interpret 2D video data to describe qualitatively the characteristics of a participant's movement in three different walk types and wearing three different garment types. The four LMA components can be described as follows: analysis of Body involves determining body part usage such as initiation, connection, and sequencing. Space analysis is the person's use of their body in the surrounding space, which includes whole body use, interaction with the environment, and personal space. Shape elaborates the forms, or changing forms, that a person's body makes in space. In this category, Shape Quality provides a set of descriptors for dynamic shape characteristics, such as spreading or enclosing, rising or sinking, and advancing or retreating, outward–inward, upward–

downward, and forward–backward in motion. Basic Shapes, in the Shape analysis category, describe the static shapes that the body takes, for example wall-like, pin-like, ball-like, or screw-like. Each of the names is defined by specific use of space along the planes of horizontal (left–right), vertical (up–down), and sagittal (up–down and forward–backward). Effort describes the expressive style of one's movement, its changing, dynamic quality and the person's inner attitude towards using energy. The LMA Effort factors have four elements: Flow, Space, Time, and Weight.

These comparative movement sequences allowed a closer analysis of the moving body in its trajectory through space and time, and also enabled an analysis of sequences, such as movement phases, postures of the body, the organization of the body and its parts, the shape of the body, and the relationship of the body to emotion. For example, in the 'happy walk', in terms of Shape Quality, there was a pattern of extreme 'spreading', 'rising', and 'advancing', regardless of the type of garment with which the participant interacted. Conversely, the 'fearful walk' patterns of movement, particularly while the participant was interacting with the 'fearful garment', were found to be extremely 'enclosing', 'descending', and 'retiring' in Shape Quality. As for Basic Shape, within this changing kinesphere, the torso changed shape from wall-like to ball-like to screw-like and gradually descended in a spinal contraction, while limbs moved towards the body's centre in a closing movement. The pattern of the participant's use of Body Forms in Space signalled caution, as the participant appeared to protect the body against impending danger. In this pattern, her body shape expressed enclosing, descending, and retiring movements.

These two quantitative and qualitative kinaesthetic experiments resulted in four significant essential considerations and principles for the design of a garment that is functional while enabling expressive movement across a range of emotional situations.

1   ***Kinetic variation of self-awareness***: this refers to our bodies knowing consciously and unconsciously how to adapt an object for comfort in insecure or secure, or various other, emotional situations. When a participant moved their body they demonstrated spatial characteristics in response to whether they were placed in happy or fearful situations, including how far they moved from openness to closedness, from rising to descending, from advancing to retreating. For example, the way a garment is worn indicates important

emotional cues visible through the position of the trunk, head, and arms, and spatial features such as the degree of openness and closedness. The participant's use of an open body form exhibited a characteristic akin to 'showing off'. Body forms that emerged while a participant was interacting with a 'happy garment' could be linked not only to an expression of happy emotions, but also to the person's self-assured or self-centred characteristics, shown in the way a person chooses to present the body to the world (Hackney 2002). Conversely, the participant's use of closing (including enclosing, descending) body forms indicated they were wary or in need of escape, or protection from danger or fear. This expressive body form can be linked not only to the expression of fearful emotions but also to a person's introverted personality (ibid.).

2 **Kinetic variation of scale**: this refers to the variations of scale (from small to large) in how women produce different patterns, dynamics, and qualities of movement. The scale variation for designing a garment for movement is not a size differentiation, but is related to the use of personal, social, and public space. For example, the space created by the inside zone of clothes can be referred to as the 'personal, inner' space, a place to hold and protect oneself emotionally. This perspective relates to privacy and security and can be an important clue to determining how a 'happy garment' needs to accommodate emotional comfort in personal space (kinesphere).

3 **Kinetic variation of speed**: this refers to how the speed of everyday walking brings sharply into focus how our body organizes itself when walking, and how the act of walking relates to the design of a garment to allow for a balance of weight shift. For example, when wearing the 'happy garment' or 'fearful garment' a participant's hands and arms were more actively or passively engaged in the garment while walking, which manifested in slower walking and slower bodily expression (such as speed of changing position).

4 **Kinetic variation of transitional emotions**: this refers to how the emotion women experienced could change within an interactive process. With negative emotions, especially fearful states, specific fear-related action tendencies are activated, such as the preparation for concealment in order to protect the body. The process of interacting with the garment, in which it is formed, reformed, or deformed iteratively through space, means that the garment can empower forms for the body and for its covering, to construct a third skin. The participant's experience of fear was transformed into calm through the

creation of a personal space when the body was enclosed within the garment. The results indicate that the garment can have an important protective function and provide a habitable shelter in secure or insecure spaces. The protective function of clothing is not restricted to physical protection in certain climatic and environmental conditions. It extends to protecting the wearer against both physical harm and psychological dangers, whether under attack or suffering feelings of insecurity.

Design approach

The garment designs 'Disguise-Garment' and 'Jigsaw-Puzzle' were developed for movement-based interactions that responded to emotions. Using a process of designing, building, and testing, the garments were made so as to be highly experiential and interactive, so that they increased the sensorial, emotional, and functional experience.

Figure 8.5: Disguise-Garment, made from engineered felted wool embedded with LED lights. The garment is designed to protect the body as a therapeutic aid that can change the mood of the wearer.

Disguise-Garment is designed for body movement within space, where the dynamic form of the garment needs to change and be changed to adapt to a person's mood and emotion, to provide a sense of psychological, physical, and emotional wellbeing. Disguise-Garment is the second iterative design developed as a result of the observations of and interviews with a group of participants who engaged in the manipulation of the textile piece 'Trans-For-M-otion'[2] (Jeon 2012). The participants in this study were observed to be more aware of the textile forms when they were placed in fearful and insecure situations, and in response, the design concept evolved from the following research questions: how do feelings of fear or threat in insecure situations turn into comfortable, enjoyable, and playful emotions; and how does the experience of the garment act as a mood-altering material when stimulated by cognitive image processing?

The design process for Disguise-Garment focused on a fictional scenario of 'using a garment to disguise the body like a ghost' in insecure situations. Some of the women I interviewed and observed while they interacted with a garment in insecure situations wanted to be able to disguise themselves or hide their identity, so I designed the garment to be pulled upwards so that the collar could conceal parts of the face. In addition, in a situation where a threat from the rear is imminent, the garment's built-in LED light with electronic vibration is generated. In this situation the garment enables the wearer to find out how feelings of fear or threat can be transformed into comforting emotions. Therefore, the garment, with its mood-altering material, can be used as a self-help therapeutic tool. In addition to its protective qualities, the garment creates a feeling of playfulness. Created from felted wool layered units that trap air, and embedded LED lights and sensors, the illuminated garment is designed to morph and change colour to help the wearer feel simultaneously protected, playful, and confident (Figure 8.5).

The second design, Jigsaw-Puzzle, is an adaptable and transformable form that was developed to accommodate the wearer's needs in a day-to-day and moment-to-moment environment. The garment was created to answer this research question: how can a garment allow people to be functionally and emotionally adaptable when making their own stories through bodily interaction?

Jigsaw-Puzzle enables women to feel, move, and configure a garment for their own body comfort. In this sense, the garment is not centred on the functional mechanics of comfort, but the emphasis is placed on narrative use – that is, how the form is performed, felt, and configured and how its meaning of comfort is experienced by individual bodily interactions. The garment is designed to be highly experiential, so that it may enrich, inspire, and strengthen an individual's identity, sense of self, and personality. Accordingly, the function of the garment was designed to be rich and intellectual, existing not in a final material form, but as a garment open to experience.

The design of Jigsaw-Puzzle (Figure 8.6) is based on the idea of less matter but more experience, and less designing but more interaction with the body through movement and space. The garment is a geometrical drawing within a rectangular

Figure 8.6: The Jigsaw-Puzzle garment, designed to open our experiences in everyday activities.

Photographer: Kyunghoon Kim.

shape, mounted on felted wool. Multiple cut Jigsaw-Puzzle pieces can be used to create various forms – such as a hat, or a long or short sleeve jacket – or can be transformed to fulfil an entirely new function, becoming, for example, a chair. The interlocking geometrical shapes are cut to fit together and can form a big rectangular shape like abstract art. The created form is abstract, malleable, and incomplete. The form is ongoing and changeable to suit the physical and interactive needs of the body. However, the form requires the wearer's bodily interaction, since it is only through a process of manipulation that the wearer is able fully to use and enjoy the piece. The form is only considered to be complete once the wearer has determined its shape and size.

In addition, the fact that the garment is designed to be very abstract means the wearer is able to bring to bear her basic perceptual capabilities. These abilities mean that she is unconsciously drawing on her experiences and thoughts of wearing, by responding spontaneously with the garment in the space. The garment evokes imaginative experiences, where the wearer creates an ideal form through feeling and thinking, and intuitively through bodily movement. In the observational study the participants had a clear idea of what, when and how comfort was required and they and their bodies became idea generators in the design development process. As a transformable garment, Jigsaw-Puzzle performs an experiment with space and construction. It allows the wearer to refine and maximize the wardrobe beyond its usual wearable potential, by transcending established boundaries and challenging the conventions of fashion. The garment becomes enriched with interaction and becomes garment-less as it moves beyond traditional forms.

Research outcomes

This research-through-design project explores the phenomenological way women touch, move, and feel when they participate in enriched and dynamic bodily interactions by tactile (haptic) experience, kinaesthetic phenomena, and emotion. It reveals how the unity of haptic, kinaesthetic and emotional elements can influence a new form of garment design and performance. From this research, three important reflections have emerged.

1   First, it is worth noting that a sensorimotor-driven design approach, such as the use of dynamic modes of touch in garment design, could assist people to elicit senses and positive emotions that can modify their negative affective

states so that they become positive emotions or moods. Designers should give greater consideration to the significance of the touching process, and engage this with an interactive design process.

2   The second reflection I emphasize is that investigating movement within the garment, as one of the kinaesthetic elements of bodily interaction, offers a way of understanding the particular role of 'movement' in human–object–emotional interaction. New forms can emerge when exploring body movements and identifying properties of comfort that occur in bodily interactions between people and their environments, especially when observing how a body is shaped and patterned, or how people wrap their bodies as part of their wearing behaviour. This methodology offers insights into how a garment can be designed precisely to adapt to people's body movements and bodily transformations in an environment where moods and emotions are constantly changing.

3   Finally, my design strategy stresses that the garments I design invite people to participate actively in forms that create sense and meaning. The garments require the wearers to interpret and interact with the form within the space they inhabit, but how they wear, interact with, and appropriate the garments is left open to individual experience. My garment designs intend to evoke people's emotions by challenging their wearing experience, stimulating their imagination, and enhancing their interaction practices rather than concentrating on style, visual expression, and appearance. Accordingly, my garment designs empower users to think, raise their sensory awareness, and provoke them into action.

Conclusion

Clothes are an extension of our bodies – we regularly wear, desire, possess, store, inherit, and discard clothes. Within the life of a body, clothes are essential contributors that adorn and protect the skin. When a garment invites touch and movement; when it evokes emotions; when it triggers nostalgic memories; then it enables people better to appreciate the objects they interact with and their environment. The garment that helps people to appreciate these small differences enhances the physical and psychological benefits from interacting with objects, helping to relieve depression and increasing a general sense of wellbeing. These objects and clothes offer a new form of rich aesthetic interaction to the user.

Notes

1 This research is based on the doctoral thesis titled 'Designing Enriched Aesthetic Interaction for Garment Comfort' (Jeon 2012). This research is linked to the ARC Linkage project 'Innovative Solutions for Wool Garment Comfort through Design' (Project ID: LP0775433), in conjunction with the Wooldesk at DAFWA (Department of Agriculture and Food, Western Australia).
2 'Trans-For-M-otion' is a textile development of the concepts of 'formlessness' and 'shape change'. This concept is proposed as a tool to enhance and explore self-expression and self-therapy. The idea can help people to accommodate the form for their needs – for body movements and for adapting space. In other words, for the individual, this could be used as a form of self-therapy and aid in self-awareness. It can be used expressively by highlighting an emotional state so that behaviour can be adapted accordingly.

Bibliography

Craig, J. C. and Rollman, G. B. (1999) 'Somathesis', *Annual Review of Psychology*, 50, pp. 305–331

Deleuze, G. (2003) *Francis Bacon: The Logic of Sensation*. London: Continuum

Gibson, J. J. (1966) *The Senses Considered as Perceptual Systems*. Westport, CT: Greenwood Press

Hackney, P. (2002) *Making Connections: Total Body Integration through Bartenieff Fundamentals*. New York: Routledge

Hummels, C. and Frens, J. W. (2011) 'Designing Disruptive Innovative Systems, Products and Services: RTD Process', in Coelho, D. A. (ed.) *Industrial Design – New Frontiers*, Rijeka, Croatia: InTech, pp. 147–172

Jeon, E. (2012) *Designing Enriched Aesthetic Interaction for Garment Comfort*, unpublished doctoral thesis. Perth, Australia: Curtin University

Laban, R. (1960) *The Mastery of Movement*, 2nd edn. London: McDonald and Evans

Merleau-Ponty, M. (1962) *Phenomenology of Perception*, trans. C. Smith. London: Routledge & Kegan Paul

Montepare, J. M., Goldstein, S. B. and Clausen, A. (1987) 'The Identification of Emotions from Gait Information', *Journal of Nonverbal Behavior*, 11, (1), pp. 33–42

Chapter Nine

Fashion design and disability

Kate Carroll, North Carolina State University, USA

Fashion is an additive art. Fashion designers create products to be worn or carried on and around (and sometimes within) the body. Through fashion, a body is covered, protected, decorated and transformed in varying degrees, depending on the needs and desires of the wearer. Fashion assists people in determining their physical interface with the world. It aids self-expression and can make life happier and more fulfilling. All these aspects of fashion are relevant regardless of a wearer's physical ability. Traditionally, the commercial fashion world has focused on a particular wearer type – young, slender, physically attractive according to societal norms, and able to understand the nuances of a product. Retailers who market and sell fashion products tend to focus on this customer since they are in fierce competition for their disposable income and patronage, and the supply chain has been tooled for success with this customer in mind.

For the fashion consumer who is differently abled, either temporarily or permanently, the fashion world is a remote concept as regards product options, marketing and the retail environment. Thousands of individuals struggle daily to find clothing which fits and is comfortable, affordable, accessible, aesthetically pleasing and accommodates self-expression. With the exception of a few independent companies working to provide accessible and functional garments, the mainstream fashion industry has ignored the voice of this consumer. In constant search for profit margins, fashion operates on a mass-market model, where the only concessions to inviduality are style, color, fabrication and some sizing choice. Consumers who are differently abled have had no place in this paradigm, as their needs are considered too specific to address in the mass market. In addition, companies' target customers, the foundation of many product development decisions, have not included customers whose bodies do not 'fit' the norm, either literally or metaphorically.

This chapter will focus on fashion for people with physical disabilities. Beginning in the early part of the twentieth century, when applied research was first carried out to explore the relationship between clothing and rehabilitation practice, the first section will set the stage with an historical analysis of significant developments in the United States. The chapter will then focus on a case study of one approach to a design problem, to give examples and life to the design and development process. Finally the chapter will conclude by looking at possibilities for progress through intelligent research and design solutions.

History of fashion and disability

In the United States, clothing began to be recognized and used as a rehabilitative tool in the 1930s. The acts of dressing and undressing (donning and doffing), were observed by medical staff in hospitals for 'crippled' children, as ways of improving physical and cognitive skills (Hoffman 1979). During the 1940s disability research initiatives continued to change from focusing on dependence to promoting independence, and clothing was seen as a critical part of this process, documented by Cardwell (1947) and Dillingham (1948). In the 1950s, mainstream designers such as Mary Brown, who, influenced by her mother's Montessori school curriculum, designed clothing for children with cerebral palsy, started to create specialized designs for specific populations, incorporating a fashion element combined with functionality. In the latter part of the decade, a prominent fashion designer, Helen Cookman, was hired by the Institute of Physical Medicine and Rehabilitation in New York to improve the design of clothing for people with disabilities. Due to her status as an established designer, she went further than helping people achieve independence. After a three-year period of study, she produced a line of 17 fashionable garments for men and women with physical disabilities, utilizing high quality 'fashionable' fabrics and construction techniques. A runway show was held to show the collection to the public at the Institute's Alumni Hall.[1] As a follow up, six of the designs were mass-produced by a non-profit company, Clothing Research, Inc. of New York City, and a self-help booklet; 'Functional fashions for the physically handicapped' (Cookman and Zimmerman 1961) was published, which included detailed pattern adaptations plus a rationale for each one explaining how it should be used to create a garment.

In 1961 Clarice Scott of the U.S. Department of Agriculture Research Service published a bulletin with detailed pattern designs for 20 garments for women with disabilities, incorporating pictures and pertinent information about construction and design details. The styles were based on first-hand research and interviews with about 70 homemakers with physical disabilities, and emphasized fashion as well as functionality, care and maintenance. The 1960s saw a huge increase in interest in this area as extension agencies developed leaflets, programs and self-help advice for dressing, grooming and comfort, and advice on how to alter ready-to-wear clothing. In 1965 Fashion-Able was founded, a company specializing in the design and marketing of underwear for women with disabilities; it became so successful that the business quickly expanded to offer a wider range of clothing products and assistive devices. Options for clothing continued to increase and in 1973, the Rehabilitation Act was passed in the USA, giving momentum to a new interest in research, mostly for individual problems as case studies. In the 1980s, attention started to turn towards fashion and its relationship to the outward self as experienced by people with disabilities, adding a psychological component to be considered in the design process, along with functionality considerations. These decades of applied research produced a broad body of work pertaining to design for disability, including lists and explanations of style features, adaptations, fabrications, construction, closures and other critical areas.

In spite of this gathering and validation of information, fashion solutions are not readily available for individuals with disabilities in a mass-market fashion environment. The greatest advances have come from a grassroots level. Entrepreneurial family members of people with some type of disability, as well as empathetic fashion designers, have provided solutions, often designing and making several iterations of a product, producing small runs with the help of local manufacturers and selling online or face to face, using word-of-mouth advertising and social media to get the word out about their products. It has been acknowledged by the mass media that people with disabilities lead varied and fulfilling lives. Television shows such as *Push Girls* and *Britain's Missing Top Model* have opened viewers' eyes to the lives of people with disabilities. But on a day-to-day level, people with disabilities still have problems finding fashion that expresses and embraces their lifestyle and personal aesthetic. Technological advances experienced by the fashion industry give designers an opportunity to move forward in their thinking about design in this area. These include advances in computer-aided design and product development; development in materials; and changes in the way that we purchase fashion products.

As of the current date, there are far fewer companies designing, producing and selling fashion for people with disabilities than for able-bodied consumers. A number of 'specialized' clothing companies, such as the Xeni Collection, Rolli-Moden and Silvert's Adaptive Clothing, successfully serve the needs of people with disabilities, offering products that range from highly functional to more fashion-oriented, mostly through online and catalogue channels. However, no mainstream retail company has stepped up to rethink product lines or the retail environment creatively, to facilitate product acquisition, in spite of technological advances made in the industry from design to purchase and consumer use.

Current industry practices

Designing fashion for people with disabilities is perceived as a different process from the design strategy for ready-to-wear fashion, where the needs and preferences of individuals are not known beyond a target market segment. The traditional ready-to-wear market is stratified using demographic and psychographic data so that satisfaction of a group aesthetic is core to the design process and eventual product success. The communities formed by people with disabilities are linked by similar demographic and psychographic parameters, and also by varied levels of physical and psychological ability, which adds complexity to the product development process from many perspectives. This presents challenges to designers and pushes thinking beyond the typical ready-to-wear design experience. Susan Watkins, in her book on functional clothing design *Clothing: the portable environment* (1984) suggests that designers of clothing products intended for customers with special needs learn about body mechanics, materials properties, basic psychology and aesthetics, so that this knowledge can be used in developing successful products.

For any fashion company, the desired outcome of good design and development is to satisfy a group of people with one brand, and to develop a variety of product lines which conform to that brand identity. The same principle can be used to address the needs of people with variations in abilities so that seemingly disparate groups can find common ground in a fashion product. An example of this might be a large buttonhole in the end of the sleeve of a long-sleeved shirt, commonly found in exercise clothing (see Figure 9.1) and in children's wear. Someone who

Figure 9.1: Woman's running top showing thumbhole at end of sleeve
Source: © 2013 Under Armour, Inc.

has challenges with internal thermal regulation might slip their thumb through the hole and use it to keep their sleeves down over the hands so that they stay warm, while another person with limited dexterity might find it useful to hook a finger through to facilitate the donning and doffing process. Designing such features into a product, which make it useful to many different populations, is a process known as Universal Design (UD). These features, initially designed to help one population succeed with a product, quickly become usable for others with seemingly disparate abilities. Universal Design, also known as Inclusive Design, and Design for All, has its roots in the built environment, but is guided by a set of principles, the majority of which are valid for development of other products. The principles and their use will be discussed in more detail later in this chapter.

An approach to the methods and processes for designing: a case study of a universally designed clothing project

This project was born from an introduction to Universal Design thinking and the growing technological advances, which facilitate flexibility in design and consumer acquisition and use. Many ideas are derived from areas outside of our general daily context, and the concept of Universal Design made its first impression almost by accident. When I was trying to find general information on disability, from physical and psychological perspectives, I was encouraged to take a class about UD in housing in 1999. I was intrigued by the challenges and opportunities afforded by a change in design thinking. I saw little difference between the application of UD to fashion or to the built environment, and began to start design projects using the principles as keystones. The principles – equitable use, flexibility in use, simple and intuitive use, perceptible information, tolerance for error, low physical effort, and size and space for approach and use – seemed applicable to clothing design to aid evaluation of the universal appeal of a product.

A traditional design workflow was followed: (a) evaluation of user needs and preferences; (b) generation of design ideas; (c) development of prototypes; (d) evaluation of feasibility with re-evaluation where necessary; and (e) implementation of changes to prepare for production. This workflow follows a ready-to-wear fashion process, such as that detailed by Wickett *et al.* (1999), but increases emphasis on the first step: evaluation of user needs and preferences. Marilyn DeJonge (1984) outlines the 'functional' design process, in which the needs of an individual user are placed at the beginning of a linear process. Other researchers have recognized the part that the user plays in the product development process. Rosenblad–Wallin (1985) first proposed User-Oriented Product Development as an approach to clothing design for people with disabilities, with the user at the core of the system. Even the Universal Design process, where the end product satisfies a multitude of users, begins with looking at individuals' needs.

(a) Evaluation of user needs and preferences

The user becomes involved in the design process from the conceptual stage of product development. In this case study, information was gathered to determine the needs of ten professional women with a variety of physical disabilities. Each woman was interviewed to determine:

- physical limitations impacting search, acquisition, wearing and care of fashion products;
- types and extent of problems with current clothing;
- practical solutions which have been found to work well on an individual level.

The methods used to gather this information depended on the type of data needed. To determine physical limitations, I felt that it was less important to categorize the disability than to evaluate how physical differences impacted clothing. The Enabler figure, developed by Mueller (1996) (see Figure 9.2), is a useful tool for this purpose. Areas of physical limitation are evaluated to determine limitations in coordination, upper body strength, head movement, stamina, sensation, lifting, reaching or carrying, handling and fingering, ability to use upper extremities and range of motion. Evaluation of each area using a Likert-type scale can help determine to what extent these limitations affect a user. In the case study, the Enabler was used during face-to-face interviews with participants and a matrix was developed to assess each individual. The interviews revealed areas of greatest limitation to be (a) upper body strength, (b) stamina, (c) lifting, reaching and carrying and (d) handling and fingering, in descending order of frequency. The participants also added comments for deeper explanation.

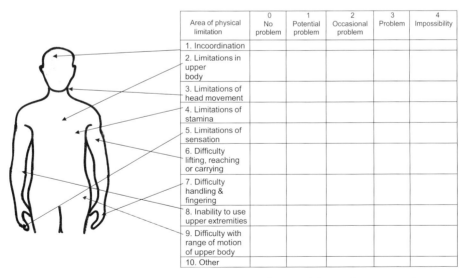

Area of physical limitation	0 No problem	1 Potential problem	2 Occasional problem	3 Problem	4 Impossibility
1. Incoordination					
2. Limitations in upper body					
3. Limitations of head movement					
4. Limitations of stamina					
5. Limitations of sensation					
6. Difficulty lifting, reaching or carrying					
7. Difficulty handling & fingering					
8. Inability to use upper extremities					
9. Difficulty with range of motion of upper body					
10. Other					

Figure 9.2: The Enabler figure and matrix used for part of the needs assessment.
Source: Adapted from Mueller (1996).

Having determined the type of physical limitations experienced by individual users, interviews were used to identify problems with current clothing. The same group of professional women was encouraged to talk about their work clothing and how it impacted their daily lives. 'Problem' areas, validated by previous literature, were as follows:

- managing fastenings★
- freedom of mobility★
- donning and doffing
- materials quality
- construction quality
- coverage of body
- details and features deemed 'irritating'.

(★reported by more than half the sample as highly problematic)

When the same women were asked about practical solutions that have helped address and alleviate these problems, the results were also similar to previous research:

- side openings and/or oversized openings
- velcro dots instead of buttons, or no fastenings
- large or oversized garments with excess fabric
- stretch and knit fabric construction
- absorbent, wicking and easy-care fabrics
- reinforced stitching in seams
- high necklines, long sleeves, raised backs on pants and skirts
- anchoring accessories and details to avoid them getting in the way.

(b) Generation of design ideas

During the case study, as problems were identified and discussed, possible solutions were co-generated by the designer and participants. Problems without a solution were set aside for further thought and experimentation. In addition, images of many of these features (tear-outs from magazines, web pages, sketches) were shown to participants so they could visualize potential solutions. This helped them to pinpoint features that they liked, but had not been able to verbalize using clothing terminology. Having established existing problems and future needs, participants were again consulted in development of design ideas for a jacket that could be worn to work. In this way a functional solution might be combined with a personal style choice based on trend forward fashion. Color charts were used to help participants determine choices, along with some basic color theory information. As choices were made the designer sketched and took notes, incorporating the ideas and features discussed. This sketching was initially done by hand but the final design was rendered in Adobe Illustrator (Figure 9.3). A flat sketch with specifications – such as points of measure, color, findings and trim, materials, construction details and order of operations – was developed. Minimal measurements were taken at the individual level (neck, chest, waist, high and low hip, center front to waist, center back to waist, waist to knee, waist to floor) and then collapsed into 'best-fit' groupings to establish a small/medium/large size run for prototype development.

(c) Development of first prototype

Prototype development involves interpreting the design sketch, making a pattern, laying out and cutting the fabric and then sewing it together according to

Figure 9.3: Flat sketch and illustration of first prototype.

pre-determined directions. The features of the garment dictated an adaptation of an upper body pattern block. The length was increased to hit at low hip level according to the median waist to hip measurement, and was widened to resemble an A-line or 'swing' silhouette. Sleeves were long and slightly funnel-shaped, so they were a little wider in the hem to echo the jacket shape. Deep pockets were patterned to be set into the side seams, a feature added to replace a purse. The jacket opened at center front and the neckline was a deep jewel shape with no collar. A long rectangular scarf was added as the only accessory. A loop was placed inside the back of the neck to keep the scarf in place. Participants could thread the scarf through the loop before putting the jacket on for ease of donning and doffing, or the scarf could be left off.

Fabric was purchased which adhered to criteria specified by the participants. A heavyweight 100 percent cotton textured woven fabric was selected for the outer shell of the jacket. The lining was a brightly printed 100 percent polyester crepe. The shell was a burnt orange, while the lining had touches of orange, purple and cream. The scarf was also created from the lining fabric. The fabric was not subjected to any testing before being chosen – it was selected according to aesthetic, weight and hand criteria.

Fabric was cut, and the prototype was stitched together to check for fit and to edit the order of operations and any other specifications which needed adjustment. The entire garment was stitched with a 5-thread safety stitch for durability. The 5-thread safety is useful in that it makes a seam and finishes edges in one operation. The buttonholes were a unique design element. Three buttons were set on the front, each with a diameter of 1.25 inches. The buttonholes were set on a diagonal, and had a keyhole end for extra security. The diagonal buttonhole had not been mentioned in the literature, but it appeared to have a shape geared towards durability and ease of manipulation.

(d) Evaluation of feasibility with re-evaluation where necessary

Two types of evaluation took place. The first was a modified wear-testing process requiring two sets of participants: one set requiring specific adaptations (Users), and one set who required no adaptations and did not have a disability (Evaluators). Due to time constraints and the limited number of prototypes developed (three), both sets of participants were brought into the lab to try on the prototype at individual appointment times. The Users were asked to assess how the prototype addressed the problems raised in the initial interviews. This process related the prototype directly back to user needs and preferences, and helped determine whether each User's needs were satisfied by the prototype. Wear-testing of a product in industry is typically done by testing a garment on a suitable model who approaches the target customer type for that company and line of products. However, this type of wear-testing may not fully measure the reality of a situation when testing for garment performance. There is evidence of low correlation between simulated 'lab' tests and long-term studies (Collier and Epps 1998), but in this case the lab test was the only option to capture reaction by both sample groups. The wear-testing was accompanied by a second set of in-depth interviews, which were designed to measure the participants' response to the garment. Precedent exists for both wear-testing and an evaluation questionnaire in assessment of functional clothing (Bergen *et al.* 1996). Wear-testing with the Users and Evaluators took place using audiotapes as back-up to researcher notes. These audiotapes were replayed to check comments against the researcher's notes during transcription. During data collection, the researcher asked for comments by Users and Evaluators in reaction to the clothing. Other comments or suggestions were noted separately. This wear-test process with both Users and Evaluators was essential when the intention was to have one outfit designed to serve the needs of a variety of consumers. The wear-test resulted in the modifying of the number of fastenings in the front of the garment from three to one.

The second type of evaluation measured the prototype's adherence to the principles of Universal Design. The evaluation was carried out by two experts in Universal Design, with no prior ties to the project. The prototype was deemed *equitable* in use for both Users and Evaluators; *flexible* as it contained a wide array of features; *simple and intuitive* as it was easily donned and doffed (however, one User and one Evaluator confused the right and wrong sides of the garment due to there being no label for guidance and the pattern pieces being exactly the same); it was put on and worn with *low physical effort* (note that the garment was only worn for about 20 minutes by each participant); *size and space* evaluations were mixed (all Users and Evaluators were content with the coverage provided and mobility allowance, but one Evaluator felt 'pulling in the shoulders' and another wished for more buttons in the center front to prevent 'gapping'). *Tolerance for error* and *perceptible information* were not assessed in this study.

(e) Implementing changes to prepare for production

At the end of the product development process, two industry personnel were consulted to assess the prototype for production feasibility. The questions developed for the interview with industry personnel came from manufacturing and marketing screening factors for new product feasibility (Cohen 1991). The process of bringing industry constraints into the framework for development of new clothing products was envisioned by Kallal and Lamb (1993) and perceived to be an essential part of the product development process. When shown the prototype and specifications, consultants immediately suggested a mass customization approach, where adaptable features (e.g. fastenings, trim, collar, cuffs) could be offered as choices from a database. Body measurements would be submitted, and a separate marker made for each User's choice of garment. Questions were raised by the engineering manager about the practicality of the situation. For example, would it be possible for small manufacturers to adopt this strategy if expensive software solutions were needed? The managers both agreed that Users with a laptop computer and suitable software could be more involved with the actual design process while ordering their choice of garment, whether the option was co-designed with a designer or mass customization. Their choices could be digitally transmitted back to production facilities for marker and pattern layout, then cut pieces for various garments would be sent together either on a modular system or a unit production system. Digital technology could be used to aid the User in visualizing the finished garment on the body, using a virtual body model.

Discussion then took place relating to the engineering and manufacturing feasibility of the proposed product. The design sketches showed a scalloped edge down the center front. Elimination of the scalloped edges was suggested due to high labor cost, and a trim was suggested as an alternative. The original sketch showed a set-in sleeve pattern, but concerns arose regarding mobility of movement with this sleeve. A raglan sleeve seemed to offer a better production solution with similar fit capacity. In addition, the raglan option was encountered previously as an accessible sleeve type for people with disabilities. This would also eliminate the need for a center back seam, which had been identified as 'irritating' by some Users during Phase One, and move seaming to the sleeve area. Consultants saw a possibility in a new generation of fasteners, which could be useful for future studies involving people who had difficulties with traditional methods (e.g. zippers, buttons). Suggestions were also made for suitable fabrics and the researcher was shown an interlining fabric that could be sandwiched between the fashion fabric and the lining to regulate body temperature. Final modified specifications for the garment are shown in Figure 9.4.

Future thoughts

The case study raised issues provoking thoughtful re-evaluation of the design and product development process, outlined as follows:

1   ***Gathering user needs:*** Alternative ways of determining physical limitations include measurement of deviations from established norms for body posture and range of motion. To determine these types of measurements, instruments adapted from fields such as industrial design and ergonomics could be used. To measure deviations in body alignment, ergonomists use goniometers, inclinometers and movement recording systems. Typically an evaluation is based on measuring the degree of angle of body part away from an established stance, such as an upright baseline. There are also established scales used to determine deviance from a norm in posture and alignment. One example of

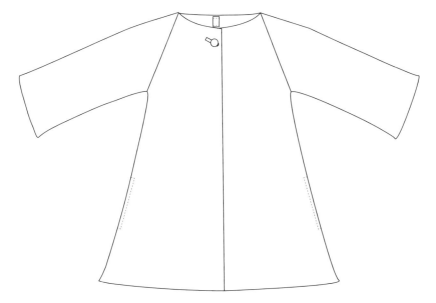

Figure 9.4: Flat sketch showing modifications post-industry consultation.

such a scale would be the New York Posture Rating Scale, originally published in 1958 and modified in 1992 (Howley and Franks). This has been used in a variety of studies, but rarely associated with clothing development or clothing for people with disabilities. However, McRoberts *et al.* (2013) used it to assess the postures of women aged 40–55 to test the development of a posture support garment. Scales like this have potential for developing fashions for people with very different postures and body types, especially when used in conjunction with a 3D body scan, which could also be used as a visual cue to determine posture ranges on the scale. These range differences would then translate into pattern adjustments to facilitate range of motion in a garment.

2   *Determining the social and psychological impact of clothing on the wearer:* Research carried out from a psychological/expressive perspective shows that many issues other than fit and physical comfort exist for people with disabilities. Fashion is used as an appearance management tool, concealing and/or enhancing, and deflecting attention from the disability. People with disabilities are interested in clothing which combines durability, comfort and fashion, although the degree of these combinations will differ according to usage context and the age of the wearer.

3   *Technological progress in fashion development and marketing:* Many advances in garment development technology have followed this project and will drive subsequent research. For example, Radvan (2013) shows how developments in seamless knitting technology can be used to address clothing needs of women with disabilities. Virtual 3D garment visualization technology enables designers to 'stitch' a pattern onto an avatar and visualize the product on the body without the need for a physical fit model in the early pattern development stages. Designers can look to physical testing of fabrics to determine the best selections for a variety of uses, such as tests for durability, and for comfort. Tests may vary between regions of the world, but determination of stretch and recovery, strength, resistance to shrinkage, colorfastness, crocking and pilling are important factors to consider when designing clothing and accessories with consistency of performance for people with disabilities. In the marketing area, consumers can use social media sites such as Pinterest to share experiences and information about new and useful products. At the time of the study, online shopping was becoming a relevant piece of the retail experience, but the ability of consumers with disabilities to interact with each other online through social media sites has now become an important part of product sharing and pre-purchase behavior.

4 ***Wear-testing:*** Standard wear-testing, where fit, comfort, usability and aesthetics are evaluated over a longer period of time such as a week, with a user being given the garment to take home and wear, would be preferable to a lab situation. In this case, they would be given a journal to document the test. Validity of wear-testing in certain situations can be increased as more variables are controlled and more explicit instructions are given.

5 ***The 'Public Face' of disability:*** Models with disabilities are becoming more prevalent. Aimee Mullins has modeled for Alexander McQueen and is also an actress, motivational speaker and former athlete. *Britain's Missing Top Model* is a popular television show documenting the lives of models with disabilities. Sophie Morgan, co-developer of the 'Mannequal', designs with Stella McCartney, and has been featured in ad campaigns. Designers with disabilities, such as Justin LeBlanc on the 2013 season of *Project Runway*, have had success as competitors on TV shows. Mason Ewing and Antonio Quistian Jr are other designers with disabilities who have broken into mainstream fashion.

6 ***Rethinking individual disability as a point on a continuum of differently abled and differently shaped:*** For example, obesity is now officially considered a disability in the USA. The design of fashions for people in larger sizes is now technically considered designing for disability. What does the future hold for designers and retailers for the plus-sized market?

7 ***Designer education:*** Fashion design education programs must strengthen this area. Schools do not offer many specialized programs but popularity and need is growing. Classes, workshops and continuing education should address these needs as part of the design education experience. Interaction with consumers at this level is essential, as many students who become involved have developed their interest either from personal interaction with someone who was experiencing some type of disability, or from their own personal experience.

Note

1 Link to the newspaper article in the *Milwaukee Journal* from Cookman's show in 1958: http://news.google.com/newspapers?nid=1499&dat=19581102&id=q0ca AAAAIBAJ&sjid=xyUEAAAAIBAJ&pg=7293,676164 (accessed 4 July 2014).

References

Bergen, M. E., Capjack, L., McConnan, L. G. and Richards, E. (1996). Design and evaluation of clothing for the neonate. *Clothing and Textiles Research Journal*, 14(4), 225–233.

Cardwell, V. E. (1947). *The cerebral palsied child and his care in the home*. New York: Association for the Aid of Crippled Children.

Cohen, W. A. (1991). *The practice of marketing management: analysis, planning, and implementation*, (2nd edn). New York: Macmillan.

Collier, B. J. and Epps, H. H. (1998). *Textile testing and analysis*. Upper Saddle River, NJ: Prentice Hall.

Cookman, H. and Zimmerman, M. E. (1961). *Functional fashions for the physically handicapped*, (Patient Publication III). New York: Institute of Physical Medicine and Rehabilitation, New York University Medical Center.

DeJonge, J. O. (1984). Foreword: the design process. In S. M. Watkins, *Clothing: the portable environment* (pp. vii–xi). Ames, IA: Iowa State University Press.

Dillingham, E. (1948). Feeding and dressing techniques for the cerebral palsied child. *Crippled Child*, 26(4), 20–22, 29.

Hoffman, A. M. (1979). *Clothing for the handicapped, the aged, and other people with special needs*. Springfield, IL: Charles C. Thomas.

Howley, E. and Franks, B. (1992). *Health fitness instructor's handbook*, (2nd edn). Champaign, IL: Human Kinetics Books.

Kallal, M. J. and Lamb, J. M. (1993). Linking industry practice with apparel design education, paper presented at the International Conference on Fashion Design, Helsinki, Finland, May.

McRoberts, L. B., Cloud, R. M. and Black, C. M. (2013). Evaluation of the New York Posture Rating Chart for assessing changes in postural alignment in a garment study. *Clothing and Textiles Research Journal*, 31(2), 81–96.

Mueller, J. L. (1996). Universal design for products. In R. L. Null and K. F. Cherry (eds), *Universal Design: Creative solutions for ADA compliance* (pp. 104–113). Belmont, CA: Professional Publications.

Radvan, C. (2013). Inclusively designed womenswear through industrial seamless knitting technology. *Fashion Practice: the Journal of Design, Creative Process & the Fashion Industry*, 5(1), 33–58.

Rosenblad-Wallin, E. (1985). User-oriented product development applied to functional clothing design. *Applied Ergonomics*, 16(4), 279–287.

Watkins, S. M. (1984). *Clothing: the portable environment.* Ames, IA: Iowa State University Press.

Wickett, J. L., Gaskill, L. R. and Damhorst, M. L. (1999). Apparel retail product development: model testing and expansion. *Clothing and Textiles Research Journal,* 17(1), 21–35.

Chapter Ten

Illuminative smart fashion

Jin Lam, Institute of Textiles and Clothing, Hong Kong Polytechnic University
Joe Au, Institute of Textiles and Clothing, Hong Kong Polytechnic University

Introduction

As wearable technology becomes more commonplace, it is changing our perception of human subjectivity, creating new concepts of identity, new systems of behaviour and extensions of the body itself.

> Cloth has always acted as an interface between the body and the external world. Wearables are no exception. They offer ample opportunities for the creation of intelligent clothing that perform[s] functions according to the body's needs and requirements, and that adapts to the environments.
>
> (Tao 2005: 9)

In present times, contemporary fashion is a lifestyle consumer product that is able to convey the wearer's thoughts and beliefs to other people. With the help of modern technology, fashion designers now play an important role in strengthening an individual's ability to express his or her unique identity in society (Chui *et al.* 2009). This chapter discusses smart wearables through a case study of the 'Illuminative Smart Fashion' project, which aimed to develop high value fashion garments that are able to sense and react to the changing environment by means of visual communication.

According to the study 'A roadmap on smart textiles' conducted by Schwarz *et al.* (2010), the fashion and clothing sector acts as the most promising application among the clothing, interior and technical textiles industries for smart fashion and textile products. There is a steady growth of smart fashion and textile products in the market because of increasing consumer needs and demands for an improved quality of life. These smart products are vital for individualisation in mixed societies that are full of diversity and differing personal lifestyles, because smart products can be used to improve interpersonal communication and interaction. In particular, this includes light-emitting and colour-changing fashion and textile products, which are capable of allowing wearers to express their own identities in new ways. 'Fashion can also play an important role in helping to construct and communicate personal and organisational identity through display' (Smart Textiles Network 2006: 2).

Definition of the smart fashion and textile system

There are many ways of attempting to define or describe smart wearable products. Tao (2005: 2) describes the generic system design of a wearable electronic or smart textile system as requiring five basic functions, namely 'interface, communication, data management, energy management and integrated circuits'. Schwarz *et al.* (2010: 107) define a smart fashion and textile system as the intelligent material or system that is able to sense and respond to its surroundings in a practical and predictable way, with the major functions of 'sensing, actuating, powering/ generating/storing, communicating, data processing, and interconnecting'. Byluppala *et al.* (2011: 11) also suggest that smart or intelligent textiles interact and respond to their environment and those responses 'can be either a visible change in the material's properties or result in communicating the environmental trigger to an external read out'. Baurley (2004: 277–278) further state that intelligent fashion and textile products are the tools for: a) 'remote interpersonal communication' through the huge range of 'tactile qualities (cool/warm, hard/ soft) as well as acoustic properties, having certain effects on the way people feel and respond to them'; b) 'social interaction and social gaming' by 'changing the visual appearance (colour, pattern), tactile quality or shape of the clothing', so 'people can interfere and interact with the clothing of others in the vicinity'; and/ or c) 'creativity and gaming' by 'allowing the user or wearer to customize the visual appearance (colour, pattern), tactile quality or shape of the textile, thus, giving the wearer a sense of self-expression'.

For the purposes of this chapter, the 'illuminative smart fashion' in the case study is defined as smart fashion garments that are able to sense changes in the environment in terms of proximity, heat, sound, humidity and pressure, and to respond to those changes by means of various types of visual communication.

A case for the illuminative fashion garment

As contemporary fashion plays an important role in enhancing socio-cultural communication between different people, this practice-based research study combined the theories of wearable technologies, practical concept development and physical prototyping of wearable technologies in creating high value fashion design. Explorations focused on investigating how emerging technologies could facilitate various visual expressions through fashion garments. Moreover, the practical work included a hands-on study of enabling technologies through the development of a pair of illuminative smart fashion prototypes.

From a review of current illuminative fashion products in the market and illuminative features in visual communications, it was possible to determine the wearable technologies that helped to realise a conceptual experience. These were identified as a) the technology of illumination; b) the application of various sensors and wireless communication devices that could be integrated into fashion; and c) the specific circuit design suitable for fashionable garments as well as the aesthetic requirements of contemporary clothing.

This research study was practice-based in nature and the design process model of developing illuminative smart fashion was based on the concepts of 'analysis–synthesis–evaluation' found in the field of architecture and industrial design, fashion and textile design. The creative process involved the following procedural steps: a) problem recognition; b) identification of sub-problems; c) conceptual design; d) creation of individual solutions; e) combination of sub-solutions into alternative designs; f) development of prototypes; g) evaluation of prototypes; and h) detailed design with specifications. The final illuminative smart fashion prototypes were then created as an outcome of this practice-based research study.

Detailed design with specification for illuminative smart fashion prototypes

After making an assessment of the different criteria needed to develop the smart fashion prototypes in this study, a detailed design brief was established, which focused on: a) silhouette of garments; b) coloration; c) graphic pattern; d) fabrication; e) illuminative material; f) circuit layout design; g) sensors; and h) wireless communication devices. The intention was to create a pair of fashion prototypes that were able to react and present various types of visual communication as a consequence of changing environmental factors. This included developing tailor-made electroluminescent panels that responded to proximity, sound, heat, humidity and pressure sensors, and wireless communication devices. The following sections detail how the prototypes were designed to accomodate the technological requirements.

Developing the garment silhouettes

The silhouette of garment prototype 1 was inspired by the 'Giovi' wall lamp, which was designed by Achille Castiglioni and manufactured by Flos in 1982. The silhouette shared the same wedge shape profile as the 'Giovi' lamp when placed on a ceiling. The shape of the extended shoulders was created by folding the hemispheric front reflector so that it met the upper portion of the centre front. At the same time the shape of the torso panels referenced the wedge shape profile of the 'Giovi' lamp when placed on a vertical wall. The silhouette of garment prototype 2 was inspired by the 'Moni' wall lamp, also designed by Castiglioni and manufactured by Flos in 1982. The silhouette shared the wedge profile shape of the 'Moni' lamp when placed on a ceiling. By manipulating the circular front reflector, the shape of the extended shoulders was developed, and the panel of each shoulder began at the front waistline and ended at the back waistline. Moreover, the shape of the torso panels reflected the wedge shape side profile of the 'Moni' lamp when placed on a vertical wall.

Coloration

The coloration applied in prototypes 1 and 2 included five major colours – white, blue-green, yellow, blue and pink – which were placed in distinct areas of the fashion garment (Figure 10.1). Using different electroluminescent panels the five selected colours flashed to communicate visually changes detected by the garment in proximity, sound, pressure, humidity and heat of the surroundings. The white colour was illuminated when there was a change of proximity. The blue-green was used to show a change of sound pressure. The yellow presented a change of pressure or force. The blue colour showed a change of relative humidity. Finally, the pink demonstrated that a temperature change had taken place.

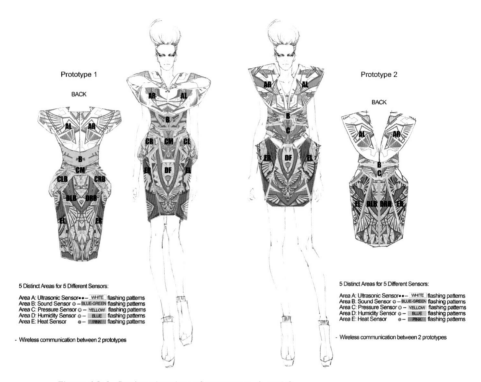

Figure 10.1: Design sketches of prototypes 1 and 2.

Graphic pattern

In order to create a design harmony within prototypes 1 and 2, the graphic patterns developed for both prototypes reference the structural drawings of the 'Giovi' and 'Moni' wall lamps designed by Achille Castiglioni. Each electroluminescent panel was divided into three zones. The flashing pattern was confined to start in a specific position and direction, moving from zone 1 to zone 2 and then to zone 3, in order to present a distinct visual display of animated graphic pattern. The detailed design sketches of prototypes 1 and 2 are shown in Figure 10.1.

Fabrication

A 0.5mm transparent PU material was used in the fabrication of prototypes 1 and 2. It served a dual function as both an interlining and a lining that provided a perfect support for the electroluminescent panels that were applied on the surface of the smart fashion garment. The same PU material, in various thicknesses, was examined carefully to meet issues of compatibility with the electroluminescent panels, in terms of avoiding stiffness and providing flexibility for bending. The selected PU material was of almost the same thickness as a single electroluminescent panel. Moreover, due to its excellent isolation performance in terms of electricity current and heat, the PU material would not interfere with the working conditions of the embedded electronic components such as electroluminescent panels, various sensors, signal transmitters and receivers. A transparent PU material was selected because this enabled the designer to assemble the electroluminescent panels and smart system on the material with better visibility.

Illuminative material and applied integrated circuit design

In total a set of 11 and 9 tailor-made electroluminescent panels were required for prototypes 1 and 2 respectively, and each electroluminescent panel had its own particular colour (Figure 10.2). The circuit design used in the electroluminescent

Figure 10.2: Tailor-made electroluminescent panel.

panel was based on the technology of flexible printed circuit board. The use of an integrated circuit design provided a reduction in wiring and mechanical connectors, thus the size and weight of the panels were reduced. However, the most important issue was the use of a highly flexible circuit design that was able to connect separate illuminative areas in a single electroluminescent panel with complex graphic patterns.

On each electroluminescent panel there were illuminating areas and a 1cm edge for installation on the fashion prototype. Each illuminating area was divided into three irregular zones. The electroluminescent panel required an electroluminescent driver, which was a high-voltage output device that converted direct electricity current to the alternative electricity current used specifically to drive electroluminescent panels. When the electroluminescent driver activated the corresponding panel, zone 1 would start sweeping light from one particular edge, reaching the opposite side within two seconds. After zone 1 had been fully filled with light, the sweeping light would pause for 0.5 seconds and then go on to fill zone 2. The sweeping light would continue in the same manner until all the illuminating areas were lit. Sweeping the light in this way was managed by further cutting each zone into a certain number of areas. Activating each area one by one would make the light sweep smoothly when seen by human eyes. Starting at the centre line, the flashing pattern would then smoothly spread to the left and right sides of the garment. Since the different illuminating areas of zones 1, 2 and 3 operated on different electroluminescent panels, the electroluminescent driver design could not be shared among all the panels. The driver needed to be designed according to the illuminating areas of each zone; therefore if the zone area was large, more frames would be inserted in order to make the light sweep more smoothly, and vice versa.

Electronic system design

The electronic system design embedded in prototypes 1 and 2 served two major objectives. The first objective was to initiate particular flashing sequences on the electroluminescent panels generated by proximity, heat, humidity, sound and pressure, which required a tailor-made circuit board and a specific sensor for each type of detection (Figures 10.3 and 10.4). When the output of the sensor met the preset condition – for example, 40°C was the preset temperature of the heat sensor – the sensor would trigger the electroluminescent driver and the flashing would

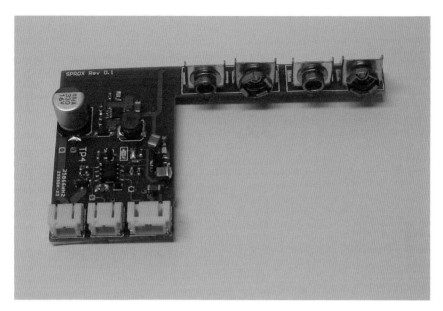

Figure 10.3: Tailor-made circuit board for proximity sensor.

Figure 10.4 : Proximity sensor.

begin. When the temperature dropped to below 40°C, the flashing would stop simultaneously. The second objective of the electronic system was to initiate the flashing sequences of the corresponding electroluminescent panels on another fashion prototype by using wireless transmission. For instance, when the heat sensor in prototype 1 detected that the temperature was above 40°C, the sensor would not only give a signal to its own connected electroluminescent driver, but would also activate the wireless communication link between prototypes 1 and 2. When the wireless module on prototype 2 received the signal sent by prototype 1, the corresponding electroluminescent panels of prototype 2 would also activate and flashing would start, until the temperature detected by the heat sensor in prototype 1 was below 40°C.

Interactions between illuminative smart fashion prototypes

The 'smart fashion prototypes' were well developed to detect the changing environment in terms of proximity, sound, heat, humidity and pressure, and to react to such stimuli by means of visual communication. The following section will discuss how the prototypes worked in terms of the detection process, and in particular will describe the interactions that were created between the two prototypes.

Proximity detection

The process of interaction between prototype garments 1 and 2 when the proximity detection is activated is described in the following scenes (Figure 10.5).

Scenes 1 to 3:

During operation, the electroluminescent panels of prototypes 1 and 2 were off when no objects were detected by their proximity sensors. When prototype 2 sensed the movement of its wearer, for example a movement of the hand (within a distance of between 0.1m and 1.5m), the garment's white electroluminescent panels started to flash; this then activated the wireless transmitter to send a specific signal relating to proximity to the other prototype garment, number 1. When the prototype 1 garment received the corresponding proximity signal, its white electroluminescent panels were activated and started to flash too.

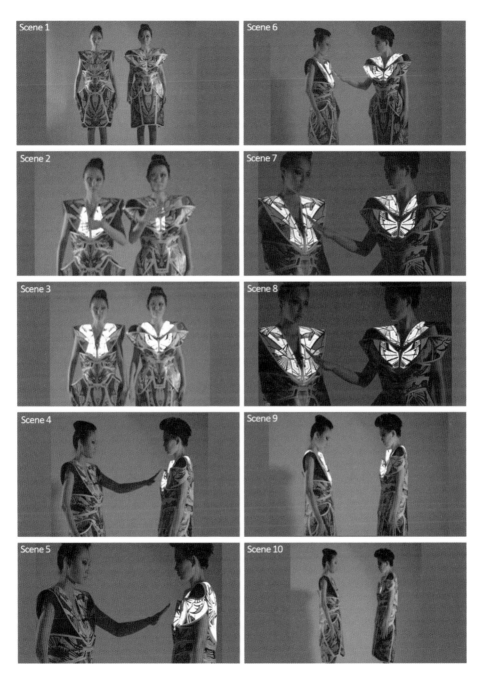

Figure 10.5: Interaction of proximity detection between prototypes 1 and 2.

Scenes 4 to 8:

When prototype 1 sensed the hand movements of the wearer of prototype 2, the white electroluminescent panels of prototype 1 started to flash. At the same time, when prototype 2 sensed the hand movements of the wearer of the prototype 1 garment, the white electroluminescent panels of prototype 2 also started to flash.

Scenes 9 to 10:

When no more object movements were sensed by either prototype 1 or prototype 2, both of the white electroluminescent panels switched off.

In a similar way, the sound, heat, humidity or pressure detection sensors were activated when triggered by their default values. Then their assigned electroluminescent panels would start to flash and a wireless signal would also be sent to trigger the other garment's corresponding panels, which would start to flash too. For example, the blue-green panels were activated by a sound pressure greater than 50dB; the pink panels started to flash when the temperature was above 40°C; if the relative humidity was higher than 80 percent, the blue panels turned on; and when an external force was applied on the pressure sensor, the yellow panels began flashing.

Findings of study

A pair of smart fashion garments that were able to sense, react to and present various visual communications resulting from the changing environmental factors (namely proximity, sound, heat, humidity and pressure) was created systematically. This development realised the design concept of integrating into a single contemporary fashion prototype huge areas of illuminative material producing complex flashing patterns with tailor-made circuit designs, a miniature wireless sensor network which detected and reacted to different stimuli, and two-way wireless communication between the prototypes.

Possible uses and benefits of smart fashion

With their capability of producing large complex flashing patterns in different colours, the developed smart fashion prototypes can be employed in the area of consumer entertainment, in stage performances. Stage performances could be enhanced through mediated environments, where the setting of the venue is also active. In a mediated environment, the wearer could present fantasies and stage performances in which the colour and animated graphic patterns changed, and the changes were then detected and sent to other garments, as the surroundings altered.

Due to their expressive visual communication, the developed prototypes are able to reinforce people's sense of identity, body image and self-presentation, and to provide novelty in the contemporary fashion and textile industry. Each prototype facilitated: i) the sending of visual messages in various animated graphic patterns in response to changing environmental factors; ii) the expression of other aspects of human communication, complementing the existing human communication channels; and iii) the individualistic wish to differentiate oneself and to declare one's uniqueness.

Because of their special features, the developed prototypes can be utilised in different fields of safety and protective garments. Since they can sense different environmental factors, present various animated patterns and send corresponding signals to another garment, they can be used to detect potential dangers in the environment and alert the wearers to various environmental conditions. In addition, they can assist people with sensory impairments to make appropriate responses to different environments. The visual messages in various animated graphic patterns generated by the prototypes could play a vital part in helping people with sensory impairments to communicate with others when there is change to the environment in terms of distance, sound, temperature, humidity and pressure. Both parties would then be aware of the environmental changes and could plan their responses accordingly.

Limitations

The present research study has made significant contributions to illuminative smart fashion in terms of theoretical and practical developments, but certain limitations are still envisaged.

Like most of the wearable electronics developed in the field of fashion and textiles, the prototypes are not washable (Schwarz *et al.* 2010). Although the wireless sensor network and electroluminescent drivers can be removed from the prototypes, the electroluminescent panels with the tailor-made integrated circuit designs are not detachable.

Like other smart systems, different interconnections of components were linked up by electronic cables and represented problematic issues (ibid.). Although the major circuit layout designs used in the prototypes were mainly developed by tailor-made, flexible and standard printed circuit board technology, with their size and weight reduced significantly, some electronic cabling was still applied for the interconnection. This might create inconvenience and discomfort during wear.

Power is still a major issue in smart systems (ibid.). The developed prototypes required batteries to power up each sensor together with its corresponding electroluminescent driver and electroluminescent panel. According to the 'burn-out' test conducted on the batteries used in the prototypes, the batteries would only provide power for 45 minutes in full operation because of the large complex flashing patterns produced by the electroluminescent panels.

Conclusion

The purpose of this study was to combine artistic creativity and scientific rationales and principles, as well as engineering and technical know-how, to design and develop high value fashion prototypes. The 'illuminative smart fashion' prototypes were developed to sense and react to changing environments by means of visual communication. The study implemented a design process model that focused on developing and creating prototypes which could alter visually in various ways in response to changes of proximity, sound, temperature, humidity and pressure, while at the same time full consideration was given to the aesthetic requirements of contemporary fashion styling, and the technological characteristics of illuminative material, circuit layout design, sensors and wireless communication devices. This practice-based research study combined the theory of wearable technologies with practical concept development and physical prototyping to create high value fashion design that has made valuable contributions to the fashion industry, fashion education and applied research in wearable electronics.

Finally, contemporary fashion plays an important role in enhancing socio-cultural communications between all sorts of people. The desire and need to continue to develop illuminative smart fashion is important for society because:

> an intelligent world will be one in which our interactions with products become ever more intuitive, using materials and systems that are responsive to our methods of communication, such as touching and the use of body

language. Intelligent materials will improve our control over our material environment and facilitate our creative interaction with it as we seek to be co-creators, tailoring experiences to correspond to our various moods.

(Baurley 2004: 275)

In the near future, I believe that more innovative smart fashion garments will come on the market that are capable of bringing people's minds closer together.

References

Baurley, S. (2004) 'Interactive and experiential design in smart textile products and applications', *Personal and Ubiquitous Computing*, 8(3–4), 274–281.

Byluppala, M. M. R., Van Abeelen, F., Rambausek, L., Smaniotto, A. and Van den Kieboom, E. (2011) *SYSTEX Vision Paper for fostering commercialization of smart textiles in European lead markets*. Taipei, Taiwan: SYSTEX Corporation.

Chui, M., Cheng, O. Y., Yip, D. and Lee, C. P. Y. (2009) 'The elegant and motivating wearable clothing'. In A. Ferscha, G. Kotsis, D. Roggen, L. Dunne, R. Mayrhofer, A. Krüger, H. Hörtner, S. Seymour, C. Sommerer and A. Riener (eds), *Advances in wearable computing 2009*, Proceedings of the 13th International Symposium on Wearable Computers, Linz, Austria: Austrian Computer Society, 49–54.

Schwarz, A., Van Langenhove, L., Guermonprez, P. and Deguillemont, D. (2010) 'A roadmap on smart textiles', *Textile Progress*, 42(2), 99–180.

Smart Textiles Network (2006) 'Light-emitting textiles for fashion and health', workshop report of a collaborative workshop hosted by the IMI and the EPSRC Smart Textiles Network, London: RIBA, 24–25 January.

Tao, X. M. (2005) 'Introduction'. In X. M. Tao (ed.), *Wearable electronics and photonics*, Cambridge, UK: Woodhead, 1–12.

Index

Page numbers in *italic* indicate figures.

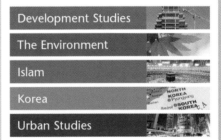